Spinach and Beyond

Loving Life and
Dark Green Leafy Vegetables

A Cookbook by Linda Diane Feldt

Forward by Suzanne W. Dixon, MPH, MS, RD

Moon Field Press
P.O. Box 3218
Ann Arbor, MI 48106-3218
www.moonfieldpress.com

Published in Ann Arbor, Michigan, United States of America, by
Moon Field Press
P.O. Box 3218, Ann Arbor, Michigan 48106-3218
www.moonfieldpress.com

Cover photo and design by Linda Diane Feldt
Line art by Shannon Berger

Printed in Saline, Michigan, United Sates of America, by
McNaughton & Gunn Inc.

Bound in Macedonia, Ohio, United Sates of America, by
Steffen Book Binders

Library of Congress Control Number: 2003111731

ISBN 0-9652132-1-8

First Edition

Printed on recycled paper

Note to the reader: For personal dietary advice and assistance, please
consult a health care professional

Dedication

This book is dedicated to Suzie Kelsey, 1972-2000.
Because she loved life, and dark green leafy vegetables.

Acknowledgments

There are many people who asked me to create this book. They deserve the first thanks for their ongoing encouragement. They are mostly my clients and students, too numerous to name. I also thank the many people who were consistent in their response to the idea of a cookbook about greens –"I'd buy it!"

My mother and grandmother had their own way of cooking, their own way of doing things, and each of us rebelled in some way against our mother's guidance, yet the deep love of food and cooking , growing plants being in nature is something we each embraced. I am grateful for that legacy.

Susun Weed, herbalist and Wise Woman, helped to reawaken my interest in wild plants and taught me most of what I know about eating weeds and wild food. Learning from Susun was life changing.

The People's Food Co-op in Ann Arbor ,Michigan has a significant role in creating this book. For more than twenty years my association with the Co-op has helped me to appreciate natural food, to learn about food choices, to have year round access to organic produce of the highest quality, and to learn and understand the value of cooperative principles. I appreciate all of the people past and present who are part of the Co-op.

Friends and family helped with tasting, testing, reading, and other support. The list includes Liz Brauer and her sons Caleb and Nico Curtis, Suzie Zick, Sarah Kaufmann, Laura Ghiron, Mike Hansen, Marion Hoyer, Laurie Feldt, Connie Brown, Joanne Motino Bailey, Jeanne Raisler, Joan Cadillac, Peter Kaufman, Carol Collins, Laurie White, Anne Benedict, and Laura Meisler.

Shannon Berger provided the exact drawings I needed. Jeff Briegel gave me unrestricted access to his printing knowledge and expertise, making the practical aspect of getting the book into print more enjoyable. Bill Zirinsky provided both timely advice as well as ongoing support for each of my book projects. On more days than I can count, Mona and Keith Moorman helped me to wear out my two Rhodesian Ridgeback dogs, by letting us play with their two Ridgebacks Django and Layla. A tired dog is a dog whose owner can write. Suzanne Dixon volunteered early on to provide a forward, and I thank her for that contribution that helps to this book to begin on solid footing.

There are many cookbooks that helped me to learn to cook, and appreciate great food. In my first ventures into vegetarian cooking, The Vegetarian Epicure by Anna Thomas and The Moosewood Cookbook by Mollie Katzen were quickly worn out and heavily stained. Laurel's Kitchen by Laurel Robertson provided a basic guide. My copy of The Joy of Cooking, a gift when I moved out of my parent's home in 1977, has been a constant reference, even as I became more and more oriented to whole grains and health food. <u>Lord Krishna's Cuisine</u> by Yamuna Devi remains a favorite, it is awesome in its comprehensive details, narrative style, and incredibly wonderful recipes.

Google.com played a huge role in this book. I did thousands of searches with Google in the process of putting together this book. Google has become more valuable than the dictionary for this writer. I love my Macintosh computer. We had a trouble free and well connected relationship creating this book.

There is a special place in my heart for someone who can give straightforward, constructive criticism. My brother David Feldt excels at this, and I appreciate him always being available to tell me where I've gone wrong. Probably even more than I appreciate being told what I'm doing right. He rightly found fault with the early drafts, and it is a better book because of his suggestions.

Editing and proofreading by David, my father, Allan Feldt, and Sherry Smith makes it possible to calmly turn in the finished product to the printer. I know there are mistakes still, that is in the nature of this sort of work. Perfection is too great a burden, and the lack of it is my responsibility.

I appreciate the trees that are necessary to create a book. Recycled paper has been used for this book and 20 trees will be planted for every 2000 books that are manufactured.

I've thanked people, dogs, websites, computers and trees. That should about cover it!

Table of Contents

Forward

In 337 BC, Hippocrates stated, "Let food be your medicine and medicine be your food." When it comes to which foods offer the best 'medicine', green leafy vegetables are among the best. The health benefits of regularly including green leafy vegetables in the diet are nothing short of miraculous. Based on the latest health research, there is no doubt that plant foods, especially green leafy vegetables, can reduce the risk of many of the diseases that plague modern people. This includes heart disease and cancer, the two biggest killers in the United States today.

Current research tells us that up to 80% of all heart disease and 30-50% of all cancers are due to dietary factors. In other words, nearly all of the heart disease and up to half of the cancers that occur in the United States each year may be related to what we put in our mouths. Consider the case of cancer, a disease that causes untold amounts of suffering. Approximately 1.3 million cancers occur each year in the United States. About one-third of these cancers are due to tobacco, with another one-third to one-half being due to diet. That means that if everyone avoided tobacco and ate well, nearly 900,000 of these cancers never would occur! Isn't it amazing to consider the power you have over your own health? It's never too late to start.

You may wonder why you should focus on green leafy foods to improve your diet. There are an incredible number of reasons to include these foods in the diet. Among the most important reasons is that green leafy vegetables are loaded with phytochemicals. Phytochemicals include vitamins and minerals, but phytochemicals are so much more than this.

'Phyto' means plant, so phytochemicals are 'plant chemicals'. If the substance comes from a plant, including vitamins and minerals, it is a phytochemical. However, there are hundreds, even thousands, of other nutrients besides vitamins and minerals that are phytochemicals. Substances such as beta-carotene are phytochemicals too. Beta-carotene is just one of the thousands of phytochemicals that improve our health. The phytochemicals that are provided by green leafy vegetables truly are amazing. These phytochemicals do more than just fight disease, they improve total health.

Among the benefits of green leafy foods are improved body detoxification, healthier hormone balance, and better protection against oxidation. It may be hard to believe that food is that powerful, but the research proves it.

Eating green leafy vegetables enables the body to 'detoxify' or cleanse itself more effectively. The body has a natural ability to cleanse and rid itself of disease causing substances. Eating green leafy vegetables enhances this natural ability. These foods contain phytochemicals that quite literally, 'turn on' the detoxification systems in our bodies.

Eating green leafy vegetables promotes a more healthful hormone balance within the body. For example, simply adding green leafy foods into the diet can change estrogen balance. There are many forms of estrogen in the female human. Some of these forms of estrogen are more likely to promote diseases such as breast and endometrial cancers. Other forms of estrogen do not appear to promote these 'estrogen-related' diseases and conditions. Green leafy vegetables encourage the body to produce the healthier estrogens, the estrogens that appear less likely to promote 'estrogen-related' diseases.

Eating green leafy vegetables protects the body against a process called oxidation. As our bodies use oxygen to produce energy, oxygen by-products, called free radicals are formed. Another name for free radicals is oxidants. Oxidants cause oxidation, a process that damages cells and can lead to disease. To understand oxidation, think of rusting metal. This same type of process happens in the body. Green leafy foods are loaded with anti-oxidants. Anti-oxidants help stop the damage caused by oxidants. As a source of anti-oxidants, green leafy vegetables are hard to beat.

Despite this knowledge, many people still fail to meet basic goals for healthy eating. Green leafy vegetables, with their pungent, sometimes bitter flavors and their tough, leafy exterior, often fall low on the list of healthy plant foods that people eat regularly. Given the amazing health benefits of these foods, this is unfortunate.

This is where this book can help. We all owe a debt of gratitude to Linda Diane Feldt. In writing this book, Linda Diane has demystified the world of green leafy vegetables. With an understanding that most people are unfamiliar with these foods, Linda Diane has provided an invaluable resource for us all. She has addressed the need for practical and delicious ways to fix these foods. This book truly is a gift. In giving yourself this book, you will give yourself the gift of better health. It's never too late to improve eating habits and you can use this book on your journey to optimal wellness.

Eat Well, Live Well, Be Well!

Suzanne W. Dixon, MPH, MS, RD

Welcome

For many years I've encouraged people to eat more dark green leafy vegetables. It doesn't seem to be any easy thing for people unfamiliar with greens. People tell me they don't know how to cook "that stuff"– it tastes bad– it's too complicated – they buy fresh veggies and they rot in the crisper – they have heard it's better raw and they prefer cooked – they have heard it's better cooked and they prefer raw – they don't know how to select good quality greens.

Even people who love the taste, and would like to have greens be a regular part of their diet, need help with having more variety and creativity in their preparation. When people have tried the simple recipes, they became more excited about cooking with greens.

So I set out to create a definitive cookbook for dark green leafy vegetables. This book will:

- explain what is great about greens

- introduce over 35 different greens you can enjoy

- help you to learn how to choose the right greens

- provide information on how to choose, purchase, store, clean, and make ready each type of green

- provide plenty of quick and easy recipes

- inspire you with elaborate gourmet meals

- give you ideas for kids, and picky eaters

- give you ideas on how to use less prepared food and spend less money

- provide lots of ideas with each recipe for adapting to the ingredients you have on hand, and customizing for your taste

How to Use This Book

My singular goal in creating this cookbook is to help people add more greens to their diets. Greens taste great, are easy to prepare, and are invaluable for nourishing our bodies. Many nutrition experts suggest we eat greens daily, and research is proving this advice to be true for the prevention of disease.

Daily consumption may be a goal, but for many people dark green leafy vegetables are an unknown food, and the idea of eating them at all is hard to imagine.

There are a couple of approaches taken in the following pages. One is to simply add greens to common recipes. Greens don't always have to be a separate dish. Another approach is to provide enough variation that you can eat greens every day and be exposed to a wide range of flavors, textures, and experiences. And finally, dark green leafy vegetables can provide the foundation for great food. There are recipes that bring out the best in this versatile and varied ingredient.

As you begin to explore the recipes, feel free to open the book all the way. A special manufacturing process has been used to let you lay the book flat without breaking the spine, or causing pages to fall out. You may still need to find a small weight to hold it open to the correct page, but don't worry that it may harm the book.

Welcome to my kitchen

If you're someone who already cooks mostly natural foods, uses a lot of fresh and basic ingredients, and does a lot of cooking from "scratch" you'll feel right at home.

If you're still a little unsure when it comes time to boil water, are a little concerned about what happens when you enter a natural foods grocery, and feel much more comfortable with a box of frozen spinach than a freshly picked bunch of kale, you'll soon know your way around and feel right at home as well.

This cookbook is for the very beginner cook, who may need the most basic directions and advice. It is also for those who are already masters in the kitchen, and always looking for new ideas and inspiration. It is especially for the majority of people who enjoy cooking but don't want to spend too much time and energy doing it. For most people, recipes that are clear, simple, and quick are what they seek.

Make the recipes yours

Cooking can be an expression of free will. Recipes can be changed, adapted, overruled, and transformed. Many of the recipes included here have come through just such a process. Good cooks learn when to be precise in following the directions, and when to strike out on their own. With the comments and variations included with many of the recipes, you'll get a sense of how you can adapt and change what is offered. I encourage you to do that.

When you are baking, often more chemistry is involved. Leaving out baking soda, swapping out eggs to make it vegan, becomes much trickier. There are times when following the recipe really matters. You'll find the notes and comments will help to determine when to improvise, and when to stick to the instructions.

In the process of making many of these recipes, you will learn how to innovate, not only how to follow a recipe. Knowing how to be creative means you can adapt recipes for your unique preferences and taste, you can be creative with ingredients you have on hand, you'll always be able to find something you like to eat, and any fear or anxiety you may bring to food preparation will be gone.

What is missing

I've always heard that you should write what you know. So I've left out parts of cooking that I don't have experience with. I have used a microwave less than a handful of times. So I don't have any recipes that include microwaving. I assume that if you are an experienced microwave cook, you'll know how to adapt these recipes to fit your cooking style. I've been doing the reverse for years – if a great looking recipe includes microwave steps I figure out how to do it with a conventional stove.

This book has a clear bias towards unprocessed, natural, healthy food. White flour products, prepared ingredients, and processed foods are minimized. Hopefully these recipes will demonstrate a real alternative, while preserving great taste and easy preparation.

Salt is missing from many recipes. While salt is a welcome and important ingredient in cooking, it is often overused to hide a lack of taste. Greens rarely need much salt, their mineral rich taste satisfies – once you've broken the habit of salting food. Salt added at the table gives everyone more individual choice, and a little goes a long way.

You may also notice the nearly total absence of generic vegetable oils, margarine, and other fats for cooking. Olive oil, and occasionally butter and sesame oil are the only oils used. Olive oil is so superior nutritionally, it only makes sense to use it as the primary cooking oil, as well as in dressings, sauces, and other recipes. Have two types on hand, a less expensive organic oil for cooking and adding to recipes and a premium version used for salads and when the taste will stand on its own.

It has also been more than 25 years since I've cooked with meat. This is a vegetarian cookbook because I am a vegetarian. Some recipes use dairy products, many do not. Vegan (no dairy) alternatives are given for some recipes that do use dairy.

What is important to me is that people have a positive experience with dark green leafy vegetables. I hope that we all choose to walk lightly on the earth, aware of and responsible for our individual choices. This book reflects mine.

What matters

I encourage you to enjoy the recipes, adapt them to better reflect your choices and values, and above all enjoy the process, the chance to learn new things, and to love life and dark green leafy vegetables.

Covering the Green Basics

What is great about dark green leafy vegetables?

They taste great

With subtleties of flavor including sweet, sour, salty, nutty, bitter, and savory, these are multidimensional taste treats. They lend themselves to inclusion in other dishes providing textural and taste appeal, and can stand alone or with the addition of sauces and dressings as pot greens.

The taste of greens will vary even within varieties depending on maturity (baby greens – especially spinach – are often prized), when they are in the season (collards and kale improve in flavor after a frost), and how they are prepared (raw versus. cooked, sauteed in fat or water, steamed or baked).

The more bitter greens, including dandelion and mustard, may be an acquired taste, accomplished by starting to eat them in the spring. As the season progresses, the bitter constituents become more present in the leaves, but if you eat right along you'll get used to the taste even as the bitterness increases.

Greens have a prominence in many ethnic and traditional cuisines.

Just a few examples are Indian pureed spinach, Greek style dandelions and spanakopita, Italian pesto, and Southern collard greens. Many of the wild greens we now consider weeds were intentionally brought over to the U.S . by European settlers who valued greens for their taste, and their health giving benefits. Dandelion is one of the most prominent weeds that was intentionally imported.

These are versatile vegetables

Greens can be prepared to be eaten raw in salads, lightly steamed as a side dish, baked in casseroles, as a centerpiece in baked goods, boiled as pot greens, added to soups for color and flavor, and ground for pesto, sauces or dips. Whatever your method, the intricate, fresh and interesting flavor is appealing.

They are easy to prepare

Many recipes require just minutes to prepare. Greens are easily added to favorite recipes. Fresh greens are available most of the year, and frozen year round. Greens can be a true convenience food.

Many of them are free for the taking!

There is an abundance of edible greens in most yards and gardens, often the very plants you are removing from the garden as weeds. Dandelion, chickweed, purslane, lambs quarters, and more can all be considered free food. All you have to do is harvest it – it grows itself!

They are a great gift nutritionally

Dark green leafy vegetables contain an abundance of readily absorbed valuable nutrients. Many of these nutrients are considered essential for heart health, cancer prevention, anti-aging, support for our major organs, support for the immune system, and for overall good health. The list includes calcium, iron, potassium, folates, Vitamins A, E, B-2, B-6, C, K, biotin, magnesium, manganese, anti-oxidants and pantothenic acid.

I'm often asked what a person can "take" to prevent cancer, strengthen the immune system, be healthier, think more clearly, age more gracefully, and have more energy. The answer to all of these questions is dark green leafy vegetables. There is no other food that has more benefit for our health — and that is simultaneously being forgotten, ignored, and minimized in our diets.

There is no vitamin, supplement, magic pill, or expensive potion that can give greater overall benefits than a diet rich in dark green leafy vegetables. The answer to greater health, wellness, and prevention of disease is literally at our feet.

Where are they

Everywhere! Supermarkets are stocking more and more green leafy vegetables, both fresh and frozen. Produce stands, farmers markets, natural food stores, and specialty markets have always had them. No matter how isolated you may be, no matter your climate, you will be able to find frozen greens year round, and fresh greens for much of the year. For many people, there is also an abundance of overlooked greens in our yard and garden. These "volunteers" (also known as weeds) are sometimes the tastiest and most nutritious greens of all.

With a little planning and a bit of focused effort you can also ensure that the greens in your vegetable garden, in your yard, from your favorite food store and in your freezer are a tasty part of your daily diet.

What are they?

Dark green leafy vegetables include a wide selection of plant families, colors, style of leaves, and flavors. This informal term refers to a group of particularly nutritious vegetables, where the leaf is of value for taste and nutrition, and excluding many common salad greens that are not as nutritious. The salad greens that are low on a nutrient scale include pale greens with iceberg lettuce as a prime example of comparably low nutritional value, as well as being bland in taste.

The next chapter has more detailed descriptions of some greens that you may have already encountered, and some you'll want to look for.

How to choose them

You want plants that look healthy – minimal yellowing, fresh and crispy looking, with a strong color and no browning of the stalk or mid rib. Even if it is a variety you're not familiar with, it should look tasty – with a vibrancy and alive energy that says "eat me!". Greens that are supposed to be shiny should still have that shine in the market.

A few holes where they've already been tasted by insects is acceptable. These plants are so good the bugs love them too. Insect eggs, webs, and other signs of infestation may be a reason to pass up that plant this time.

Most greens have little obvious smell. Any chemical or soapy odors would be a reason to not choose that green. The greens may feel slightly waxy. That is natural, although wax is often added to produce to make it look shiny. If you wonder, ask a helpful produce clerk. The leaves should not be bruised, dented or smashed. This all hastens the decay of the leaf, with loss of both taste and nutrients.

Check to see where the greens are from. Local greens are probably fresher. They've traveled less distance, and were probably picked when ripe. Choose organic whenever possible (see below).

With frozen greens, you can't actually examine the contents until you've purchased the box or bag and take it home. In this case, brand name and previous experience will be your guide. Store clerks may have helpful knowledge of good brands, but your primary measure will be to buy it, try it, and remember what you like.

Why organic and sustainable matters

The term organic refers to much more than just using natural fertilizers and not using chemical pest control. Organic farming impacts our immediate environment and quality of food, as well as having a long term positive affect.

Organic food is grown in soil that is "amended" with simple nutrients including manure, compost, and the plants themselves. Destructive insects are controlled by companion planting, simple and safe repellents, timing, and having healthy plants to begin with. There is no need to use oil based fertilizers and chemicals, renewable resources are used. Many people find that the taste is better, and science has just begun to document that the nutritional benefit is greater.

For the long term, organic farming methods promote sustainability. The soil is enriched, not drained. The long term environmental impact is considered for all decision making. Crop rotation, using hardy plants that do well in the specific micro - climate they are grown in, eliminating dependency on chemical and oil based fertilizers, all have long term environmental benefits.

With the recent federal definition of organic farming, there are some smaller farms that are using the term sustainable. No matter the label, small local farming gives you the chance to learn about how the produce is grown, and make choices about the farming practices you want to support.

In many locations, organic costs more. But this may well be a matter of pay now or pay later. Many people believe that buying organic and sustainably grown produce is an investment – in lower medical costs, in support of local farmers, in helping environmental preservation. I am not advocating a decrease in donations to environmental and conservation efforts, but why is it easier to send a check for $100 to a group working for the environment, but not spend a few extra pennies to contribute at the source – buying organic foods. Your spending on organic will immediately benefit yourself and those you are feeding while also having the longer term environmental impact we all support.

To learn more about organic farming in your area ask at your natural food store, talk to the produce manager where you buy your produce, look for organic farmers at local farmer's markets, or check with local environmental organizations.

How to store greens

Frozen greens are obvious – keep frozen until you are ready to use them. A few recipes require you to thaw them in advance, and that will be noted. For those instances, thaw overnight in the refrigerator, or about three hours on the counter.

Fresh greens will last at least three days refrigerated, and sometimes up to a week. A simple sealed plastic bag in the vegetable crisper is fine. There are cloth storage bags that also work well. In a frost free refrigerator, these more open bags can hasten deterioration. In that case, be sure to use the crisper with moderate to high humidity.

Whole, uncut greens will last the longest time. As soon as the leaves are cut or ripped, they will begin to deteriorate.

You can also prepare your own frozen greens. Greens must be blanched (lightly cooked) to stop cell growth. When I have an excess of garden greens, or have harvested a bag or two of wild greens I process them all as soon as possible after picking.

As a general rule, the greens that can be cooked can also be frozen. The ones eaten raw are not likely to do well with the freezing process.

There are times you'll want chopped greens, and other times the whole or nearly whole leaf is best. Freeze them both. The recipe for blanching greens is on page 138.

How to wash them

Another advantage of using organic greens becomes apparent at this point. If your greens haven't been sprayed with chemicals, you are only dealing with rinsing off simple dirt and debris. The home removal of pesticide residue, fertilizer applications, and other contaminants is more illusion than reality.

For pesticide free greens, a simple rinse is fine. Spinach is notorious for having lot of sand and dirt on the leaves. There are a few methods for dealing with truly dirty leaves, you just need to discover your preference.

A salad spinner works, but is fairly ineffective for dirt that clings, and for leaves with texture. These spinners have a hole in the top to run water as you spin the inner bowl. The advantage is that you do end up with drier greens than the other methods.

You can also place the greens in a large bowl or clean sink. Cover with cold water, and swish around with your hands, the dirt and debris will fall to the bottom of the sink. Remove the greens to a strainer or colander to drip dry. You can also rinse each leave individually in running water, using your fingers to rub off any dirt, and exposing cracks to the stream of water so they are more thoroughly rinsed.

This step is often the stopping point for many people, as it can be tedious. I like to think of it as a meditation. It is repetitive, fairly mindless work, engaging the senses of sight and touch to examine and rinse each leaf. A perfect chore to do while meditating, singing, listening to music, or talking with friends.

How to prepare them

Should greens be cut or torn? There is a difference. Always tear when greens will be eaten as a salad, or any time they will not be cooked. When you are cooking them, it doesn't matter EXCEPT if you are preparing them in advance. If you won't use the prepared greens right away, tearing is best.

Why?

It is all about cell walls. Plants have tough cell walls – with a lot of the good nutrients protected by these walls. As soon as the cell wall is broken, oxygen enters and starts the process of decay. Cutting a leaf cuts into the cell walls. When you tear a plant, the tearing action is around the walls and they remain mostly intact. So our greens will stay fresher, with all of their potential nutritional benefit, the longer the cell walls remain intact. Heat, cutting, drying, mashing, and digestive enzymes are all designed to break cell walls.

We do eventually want the walls to come down, to access the good nutrients. We just want the breakdown to coincide with our eating. In the case of cooked food, the most destructive element to the nutrients, oxygen, is normally not introduced directly to the plant because of liquids and other parts of the dish covering the greens.

What about the mid rib, stems, and stalks? There is no single answer. Early in the spring, with tender fresh greens, these are easily edible and do not need to be removed. As the plants are older, are transported further, and later in the season, these parts may be unpalatable.

In the case of stems and stalks, just pick the leaves off and compost the rest. For the midribs, it depends on the recipe, and who is eating it. If I'm feeding people who eat a lot of greens, I leave more of the mid rib. For people new to greens, that is the part they are likely to reject.

The midrib can be removed by cutting or tearing. To cut, each individual leaf is placed on the cutting board. With a sharp knife, slice both sides very close to the rib from the leaf tip to the where the stem exits the leaf. The disadvantage of this is the time it takes, and you won't get a sense of how tender the midrib is, so you may cut out more than you need.

To rip, I hold a leaf in my left hand, folded along the midrib. While my left fingers grasp the leaf part, I tear the rib from leaf bottom up the leaf towards the tip. I'll tear anywhere from an inch to 4-6 inches depending on the type of green, how tough the rib is, what I'm making with the green, and even who I am feeding. I like this method for speed, and precision.

The midribs can be composted, or use in soup stock.

The flavors of dark green leafy vegetables

Our sense of taste is a remarkable ability. Taste actually provides us with much more information than we are normally aware of consciously. Appreciation for different tastes certainly changes as we mature, but also can be affected by disease, periods of deficiency, and imbalance in our bodies.

Many women experience cravings at different times during our menstrual cycles, so it takes little to convince women that tastes are not a constant. What women crave can signal changes, problems, and needs that women might benefit from paying attention to. Male or female, whether our bodies are responding to the changes in season, hormonal cycles, blood sugar problems, or dietary imbalances, these are good things to note.

How we respond to greens is particularly interesting, because they do contain all of the primary taste sensations – salty, bitter, sweet, and sour. Sometimes in combination, sometimes with one dominant. It would be normal to move through a range of favorite greens, as the seasons, time of the month, and nutritional needs change.

The taste also reflects some of the dominant nutritional values. Most people are unaware that you can "taste" calcium, vitamin, C, iron, and minerals. When wildcrafting greens and herbs, we learn to "taste" a plant. Tasting is a sort of testing. The poisonous plants tend to taste like poison – when a small amount is chewed in the front of the mouth, there is an immediate urge to spit it out, make a face, and sometimes even to vocalize. It becomes obvious that this is not a food plant.

Of course, wildcrafters learn before hand what are the truly poisonous plants for their area – as tasting even a small amount of a few plants can be truly dangerous. And we know some of the overt signs of dangerous plants, things like purple splotches, white berries, and of course the plants like poison ivy and poison oak that can cause strong reactions in many people. Tasting becomes an informed process, not a blind tempting of fate.

In leading weed walks, I've encouraged hundreds of people to try a variety of wild plants. In cooking for friends and students, I've placed many meals in front of people with ingredients they had never before consumed. The responses are interesting and informative.

In doing wild food walks, inevitably, at some point in the walk, I will point out a plant to taste – and emphasize that we will only taste it, please do not swallow. Even as I make the instructions clear, someone is swallowing their portion and reaching out for more. Their mouth is saying "Yes! Yes!" while the rest of the group is tasting delicately and as a group, gratefully spitting it out. The interest and, perhaps, need for what that plant has to offer overrides their compliance, overrides any concerns, actually makes the plant taste fabulous so they forget what they have just been instructed.

It is an interesting process to observe. It also shows the importance of carefully selecting which plants I invite people to taste.

Meanwhile, we can also taste the plants that provide a variety of nutrients, and watch the reaction to those as well. A plant high in calcium will have a chalky taste, feeling somewhat thick in the mouth, and could be described as bland. The presence of vitamin C is perhaps the most obvious, providing a citrusy, lemony sour taste. As anyone who has ingested wheatgrass juice can attest, chlorophyll (present in all green plants) is an intensely sweet taste. The bitter tastes may be immediately present, or come as an after taste, as saliva mixes with the plant and begins the digestive process. Bitter is the presence of minerals. Some taste this as a salty tasting green. Indeed a craving for salt can be a desire for mineral rich food.

The presence of iron is also interesting. Time after time, I have given a group an iron rich weed, such as yellow dock, and watched as nearly the whole group starts tasting it in the front of their mouth, and transfers it to their back teeth to chew. They start biting down on the green, rather than nibbling with the front teeth. The presence of iron is signaled by this chewing response. It may be why, with iron deficient anemia, there is a desire and sometimes overwhelming craving to chew ice – something that also must be accomplished with the back teeth.

As greens are eaten, not just tasted, what we experience will change. Not only are different tasting areas of the tongue affected, the plant is starting to break down. A plant rich in volatile oils, such as basil, will impart that taste with almost no breakdown needed. For other plants, the cell walls hold many of the nutrients and subtle flavors. As we chew, as saliva begins it work to break down the constituents, the flavor will change and some of the hidden tastes will emerge.

It is good advice to chew our food. As the first part of the digestive process chewing helps digestion, assimilation and utilization of the nutrients. With greens, chewing is also interesting, and necessary to realize the full flavor of these complexly flavored foods!

The Greens

While not an exhaustive list, this is enough to get you going. My personal biases and experiences are integrated into this information, your experience may be different. More detailed nutritional information can be found on the internet, in some cookbooks, and in nutritional guides. Detailed analysis of the wild greens is not always available.

Conventional Greens

Arugula or Rocket Salad
Eruca sativa

Interest in Arugula has expanded in the last decade. This bitter green adds interest to a salad, and is an attractive green often with purple tones. A small amount in salad goes a long way. It is not recommended for cooking.

Beet Greens
Beta vulgaris

Best harvested before the beets are ready, these greens have a red tinge and an earthy solid flavor. They can be used raw, in salads, as well as like chard and turnip greens. They are normally not bitter, but have a depth of flavor that holds up as a cooked green. While it can be eaten raw, it would normally be mixed in small amounts with other greens.

While all beet greens are edible, there are also different varieties that are grown for either the fruit or the greens.

Broccoli
Brassica oleracea var. botrytis

Broccoli is marginally included as a dark green leafy vegetable. It is eaten in the immature state – before the flowers fully mature. It also has great nutritional value and a mild taste. It is the dark green vegetable most often recognized and consumed by Americans. The whole stalk can be eaten. Picky eaters may peal the stalk before including it but for most recipes and taste buds that is an extra step that just takes more time. Just cut off the very end, which has partially dried and hardened, and use the rest. My dogs eat broccoli ends with enthusiasm – but they always carry them to the middle of the living room floor.

Broccoli can be eaten raw and cooked. While broccoli could be substituted for leafy greens in most of these recipes, its thicker flesh would change the recipe pretty significantly.

Broccoli is already popular and readily used. For that reason, there are no specific broccoli recipes in this book.

Brussel Sprouts
Brassica oleracea var. gemmifera

These miniature cabbages have gotten a bad reputation, and are often the subject of jokes and derision. They have a mild flavor, a substantial texture, and are best cooked. The preparation of brussel sprouts matters a lot in creating a good tasting end product. Steaming, braising, baking and stir frying are all good methods. After rinsing, the very bottom stem is removed (about 1/4 inch or less), and any yellowed outer leaves are pulled off.

For best results, make two cuts on the very bottom of the stem base, forming an "x". This allows the stem to cook more thoroughly. Without those cuts, the leaves cook so much more quickly than the tougher stem part that the result is too much contrast with soft body of the vegetable and a hard base. Brussel sprouts can also be split in half, top to stem base, a good idea for braising and stir fries.

Bok Choy
Brassica rapa chinensis

Regular and baby bok Choy is a paler green, but crisp and delicate. It has only a hint of bitter flavor, and complements almost any dish it is used for. The darker green leaves are set on a longer pale stalk, and all of it is used except for the first part where they are attached at the base. Baby bok choy is even milder, with less stalk.

Cabbage
Brassica oleracea var. capitata

Both green and red cabbages qualify as dark green leafy vegetables, and are useful for adding color, crispness, and even as the center of a meal as in cabbage rolls. Although they are not exactly dark green, their close familial relationship with the other prominent brassica family members help ensure their inclusion as a green. In the case of red cabbage, the dark green is hidden by the more prominent red color. Cabbage is good raw in salads, and cooked in stir fries and soups.

Chinese Cabbage
Brassica rapa var. pekinensis

Chinese Cabbage is one of the most mild in flavor, and tends to fade into the background of most dishes that use it. Slivered, it is nice in soups and stir fries, and can be used when a mild green is called for. It is not a good substitute for regular cabbage, even though the names are similar. It could be eaten raw, but is not very appealing unless lightly cooked.

Collards
Brassica oleracea var. acephala 'Plana'

Collards are one of the stars of dark green leafy vegetables. It has remained virtually unchanged for over 2,000 years. Perhaps because it needs no improvement. The leaves can be medium to huge in size - I've seen collard greens 16 inches across. With a high nutritional content, and versatility in how they can be prepared, collards are great to add to most meals standing on their own, in combination with other greens cooked together, they can sneak into other dishes to boost the nutrition, and the tender young leaves are eaten raw in salad. Collards vary in taste depending on the time of the year. Before the frost they have a slightly chalky taste, connoting the high calcium content, and a little sour as well, indicating the presence of vitamin C. They are mineral rich, but rarely bitter.

Endive
Cichorium endivia

Endive is known as a bitter salad green, although it is still fairly mild tasting. The young endive is nearly sweet, and the taste grows stronger as it matures. Endive is best used uncooked, but can be quickly blanched for other uses.

Fennel

Foeniculum vulgare var. azoricum

One of the stranger dark green leafy vegetables, the fennel plant with root is certainly dark green and very leafy. The root and leaves are good in combination with other greens as a pot green, alone the licorice flavor could overwhelm. All but the very bottom part of the root is great chopped in soups. It can also be sliced thin and added raw to salads. The top leafy part can be used as a flavorful garnish or addition to salads, cold pasta dishes, creamy foods, and many other occasions.

Fennel has less nutrients than most of the other dark green leafy vegetables, but provides a distinct flavor that makes it worth including.

Kale

Brassica oleracea var. acephala
There are many cultivars available including Laciniata - curly kale, Millecapitata - thousand-head kale, Palmifolia - tree kale, Ramose - perpetual kale, Sabellica - curly kale, a number of ornamental kales, and others

For most of the population, kale is what is used as garnish in restaurants. The blue-green or reddish tinged kale leaves are prettily arranged on trays, food is piled on top of it, and the kale is thrown out after the meal. Those in the know will eat the kale as well, upsetting the presentation, but benefiting from its great taste and super high nutritional value.

Kale is closely related to collards, and both are known to have persisted in their present form for over 2,000 years. There are references to these plants being used by the early Greeks, Romans, and in early European cuisine. This is no mere garnish, and deserves to be consumed as a central part of the meal!

Kale comes in many forms, including dark curly leaf, Russian fringed, lancelet, and the border plant flowering kale. Especially rich in carotenoids, kale is a star nutritionally, as well as having a non-bitter taste and does well in casseroles, soups, as a pot green, and used raw in salads.

Kale is one of the premier dark green leafy vegetables, because of its abundance of caratoinoids, vitamins, minerals, and good taste. It is without question one of the best commercial greens readily available. It is readily available year round in most groceries. It holds up well to shipping and handling, so it is rarely found frozen.

Kale grows year round in warm regions, and it can overwinter if the winter is not too harsh. It is easy to grow and have available from the garden over many months, if not year round. Frost improves the flavor, mellowing the slight bitterness. All varieties are easily grown, and they frequently reseed themselves.

Lettuces
Lactuca sativa
(oak leaf, frisee, Boston, escarole, red, romaine, etc.)

Most lettuces are picked as immature leaves. As they mature, they become very bitter. Most of them are best used as salad greens, as they do not hold up when heated. Generally speaking, the darker they are, the more nutritional value they will impart.

Most lettuces are not considered dark green leafy vegetables, because of their bland taste, paler appearance, and having less nutritional value than the darker greens. Still, they have their own value as a base for salads, and as a starting place for people just exploring greens.

Mache
Lamb's Lettuce
Valerianella locusta

This small leaved plant is described as having a slightly sweet flavor, as well as a little nutty. The leaves are "toothsome", in that they have a pleasant slight thickness. Mostly used in salads, combined with other delicate greens it makes a fine pot green, and is similar to spinach when cooked. The term "lamb's lettuce" is said to be because they shape is like a lamb's tongue. Because it grows low to the ground and can pick up dirt while harvested, cleaning it can be time consuming.

Mustard Green
Brassica juncea

The flavor of mustard greens ranges from sweet to hot. Spring greens are milder, but they can be used both raw and cooked throughout the season. A few hot mustard greens go a long way in a pot green combination, or small pieces in a salad.

Mustards include smooth leafed varieties, curly leafed, and broad leafed. The hotness varies widely. When combined with other greens, the hot flavor is reduced.

Rapini
Broccoli Rabe
Brassica rapa var. rapa

Rapini does resemble broccoli's immature flowering heads, and taste a little like broccoli that has bolted. Best used cooked, it has a pleasant bitter flavor that is not overwhelming, yet persistent. It does well combined with other greens as a pot green, in stir fries and sautes when the other ingredients will temper the bitterness, and can be used alone when baked, combined with a dairy or tomato sauce, or used in pasta dishes.

Radicchio
Cichorium endivia

Radicchio adds color and interest to salads, and has a strong bitter taste. A little goes a long way. When it is cooked, the bitterness subsides. It can add a purple red color to potgreens, best used in combination with other greens.

Sorrel
Rumex acetosa and *Rumex scutatus*

A long leafed, delicate cultivated plant, sorrel has a characteristic sour taste. Cooked or raw, it has a pleasant mild flavor, especially in salads and soups, but is great as a green in a sandwich, as an addition to a pot green combination, or with other greens in bakes and stir fries.

It does tend to discolor and slightly gray when cooked, looking somewhat unappealing, especially when right next to a brighter green kale or other leaf.

Sorrel is not often found in stores, but is easily grown and farmer's markets would have it most of the summer and fall.

Spinach
Spinacia oleracea

As the title of this book implies, spinach is the first thought of and most used dark green leafy vegetable. A staple in cartoon, kitchen, and garden, this is a light tasting, well known choice for most. Frozen spinach is readily available, and while fresh is also common many people are put off by the careful hand washing that is required. Spinach is easy to grow. It also has the advantage of being ready to eat just weeks after planting. Spinach grows best in the cool part of the growing season, but is available most of the year.

There are many varieties of spinach available, but they are primarily divided into smooth leafed or curly leafed types. The smooth leafed is much easier to clean, otherwise the taste differences are subtle.

Each individual leaf must be carefully rinsed and inspected for dirt and sand. Because of the way spinach is grown and harvested, it tends to collect sand and dirt on the leaves. You may want to clean all of your spinach at once, so that it can be used quickly later. Once it is washed, either pat dry with a towel or spin with a salad spinner.

Spinach varies in taste depending on the maturity of the leaf, with the baby greens being especially prized for their sweet flavor.

Swiss Chard
Beta vulgaris spp.

Swiss chard is many people's favorite green. It is sweet tasting, has a buttery texture even when raw, and the mid rib is rarely tough. Chard includes a redder variety, as well as the white stalked type. Both are great additions to salads, and as part of a combination of pot greens chard tends to moderate other greens that may be bitter or hot. They are great additions to many recipes, including soups and casseroles, wherever spinach is called for, and complement the tougher greens like kale and collards.

Turnip Greens
Brassica rapa var. rapifera

Similar to beet greens, turnip greens are mild and earthy in their flavor. The greens can be used as a salad green when mixed with other greens, as well as a pleasant cooked green. Turnip greens are especially welcome as a pot green.

Watercress
Rorippa nasturtium-aquaticum and *Nasturtium officinale*

Watercresss grows along steams with fresh water. It has a peppery, tangy taste and does well in salads and as an uncooked green. It is eaten young, before flowering.

"Volunteer" greens (a.k.a. weeds)

There is a "free lunch" (as well as dinner) in your yard and in the fields nearby. Dandelion, Yellow Dock, Lambs Quarters, Pig Weed, Mallow, Wood Sorrel, Wild Grape, Virginia Creeper, Plantain, Wild Carrot, Chickweed, most of these tasty and nutritious plants are already growing in your garden. Not only have they planted themselves; they are weeds so almost no maintenance is needed to encourage them to grow!

Amaranth
Amaranthus retroflexus and Amaranthus tricolor

Amaranth is sometimes called pig weed. Amaranth's flavorful leaves come to life especially when briefly cooked (about ten minutes). If you're using leaves from later in the season, cook as a pot green for 20-30 minutes. This plant is easy to identify as it has a reddish tinge to the base of the stalk, sometimes visible only when you pull it from the ground.

It is easily blanched and frozen, and is a mild green that can be used in any recipe calling for cooked spinach or Swiss chard.

Chickweed
Stellaria spp. and Cerastium spp.

Many lawns are filled with chickweed, a great salad addition, pot green and generally useful green. It also makes great pesto. The mouse eared chickweed is best after cooking. Thankfully the plant can be eaten stems and all, as pulling the tiny leaves off would make the preparation too tedious. Handfuls can be snipped with scissors or carefully picked (leave the roots so more will grow).

The flavor is mild, fresh, and pleasant.

Chicory
Cichorium intybus

Leafy chicory is used in salads, as a bitter green. Cooking decreases its bitterness. This plant with pretty blue flowers grows in disturbed ground, along roadsides, and in open fields. There are also cultivated varieties.

Dandelion
Taraxacum officinale spp.

Over 700 species exist, of which about 100 are common. This plant was intentionally brought to North America because of its value as a liver tonic, a source of vitamin A, a diuretic, and a reliever of digestive trouble. As a dark green leafy vegetable it is also one of the many plants with carotenes that research indicates help prevent cancer. With more than five times as much vitamin A as carrots, all parts of this often neglected and for some reason vilified plant are edible. The roots can be roasted for a coffee substitute (but beware the diuretic effects), the crown is boiled as a vegetable, the leaves are a pot or salad green, and the flowers can also be added to salads. Dandelion wine is made from the flowers.

The plant can be bitter, depending on the variety but most importantly the time of year. Dandelions taste best in the spring and fall, when the bitter constituents return to the root. Some varieties are tastier longer than others. Most dandelions are too bitter once they bloom. Boil the greens, add a few to salad, put a few leaves on your sandwich, add leaves to soup or stir fry, or soak a jar full of greens in apple cider vinegar for 6 weeks for a calcium-rich supplement.

Garlic Mustard
Alliaria officinalis

Garlic mustard has attracted a lot of attention recently as an invasive plant. In my area, groups have been organized to pull garlic mustard and try and keep it from overtaking native plants.

Unfortunately, nearly all of this tasty edible plant is then destroyed - no one is eating it. Garlic mustard was intentionally brought to the U.S. because it is so tasty, and is a delicious salad green, a tasty addition to a combination of greens cooked as pot greens, or alone.

This plant does have a destructive potential, which might be partially overcome by reclaiming its place as a valuable green.

Lambs Quarters
Chenopodium album

Often described as having a "goosefoot" leaf. It grows readily in disturbed ground (your garden) and is easily identified by the chalk-like covering on the under leaf as it matures. Many people prefer this leaf to lettuce as the basis for a salad. It certainly has more nutrition, especially calcium! If left in the garden the plant can grow to several feet. With regular picking, you'll have tender leaves all summer and into the fall. What you can't eat can be blanched and frozen to enjoy all winter.

The taste is mild, and slightly chalky, indicating the presence of calcium.

Mallow
Malva Neglecta

Sometimes called Cheeses for the round fruit it produces. A little like okra in flavor and useful as a thickener, the cheese-like fruit is a fun addition to salads, and the greens can be eaten as part of a salad or an addition to pot greens. Many kids are familiar with this plant that grows in both gardens and lawns.

Nettle
Urtica dioica

Stinging nettle is one of my favorite spring greens. I pick it with bare hands, but gloves are recommended. In Michigan we harvest the top 1/3 of the plant in late May and early June, while the plant is still delicate and only about 2 feet high.

The whole stalk with the leaves is cooked for about 20-30 minutes as a pot green. Once cooked or dried, nettle loses its sting. I blanch and freeze as much nettle as I can find, to savor all winter, primarily as a pot green. Nettle is especially high in iron and calcium, and has a higher protein content than many other greens. The dried leaves are a favorite infusion (a tea steeped for many hours in a closed container).

Plantain
Plantago major

Not to be confused with bananas, this is another ubiquitous plant found in most yards, especially where there is foot traffic, as it spreads with sticky seeds that people track on dirt or grassy paths. This very common lawn weed is easily found, with broad veined leaves growing in a rosette low to the ground. The leaves can be eaten in salad or briefly cooked.

The flavor is almost mild, and tends to fade into the background when eaten with other greens.

Purslane
Portulaca oleracea

The stems, leaves and seeds of this plant can all be used in salads, boiled, or even pickled. This plant is known to be rich in iron. This is a thick leaved somewhat juicy plant, and while some people like the toothsome succulent texture, some find it unpleasant. Purslane is one of the plants containing high levels of alpha-linolenic acid, a valuable Omega-3 fatty acid.

Purslane is best in salads, but can also be lightly cooked.

Seaweed

There are many different seaweeds including a number of genera not limited to *Ascophyllum, Nereocystis, Undaria, Laminaria, Fucus, Porphyra, Palmaria, Chondrus,* and *Alaria*

The wild plants are not only the ones growing on land. Although cultivation of seaweed is increasing, it is still most often harvested in its wild form. I confess to eating most of my seaweed straight from the package, without cooking or adding it to any particular dish. For more seaweed recipes look to Asian cooking, including soups, salads, pickles, marinated, and in everyday foods. Here are a few of the more common seaweeds.

Arame is a mild seaweed, can be used in quickly cooked foods like stir fries, also raw in salad. It can also be added to soups, or cooked with whole grain pasta.

Bladderwrack can be used in soups and as a crunchy topping to grains, salads, etc. It may not be the tastiest of seaweeds, but considered by many as one for the most important for preventative health care.

Toasted dulse is a salty taste treat, either by itself or sprinkled over salads, casseroles, or grain dishes. It can also be enjoyed untoasted. Hiziki is similar to Arame, a little more nutty in flavor, best used cooked.

Many seaweeds are packaged as kelp. The lighter ones can be

eaten as is, as part of a salad, or with grains and pasta. The heavier kelp (kombu) is best cooked. It is used to thicken soups and cooked with beans to make them more digestible (less gassy).

Nori Usually the most processed of the commercially available seaweeds, it is also best known because it is used to prepare sushi. It comes in green shiny sheets. In addition to being rolled for sushi, nori can be eaten as is, some people take a sheet or two to eat a rice dish, using it like bread as a scoop for the meal.

Sea Palm is mild and pretty, making it ideal for a simple soup. After being soaked for 15 minutes to an hour, it can also be used in salads.

Wakame is another mild, if slightly tough, seaweed, soaking, cooking, all improve its texture and enjoyment as an addition to stir fries, soups, and some people even like it in salads. Alaria is used similarly to wakame, it is normally soaked before using.

Virginia Creeper
Parthenocissus quinquefolia

Virginia creeper is a five-leafed vine that can easily overwhelm everything around it. Because it grows like poison ivy, often grows near poison ivy, and has branching leaves like poison ivy, it is important to be sure you see five leaves and not three. This is not a plant to pick for those who are easily confused or distracted because you don't want to mistake it for poison ivy.

The very young leaves of Virginia Creeper are sour and make an interesting addition to a salad or change the taste of a mix of pot greens. Use only the very soft small leaves, once they mature they are too tough to eat and the stronger tannins dominate the flavor. Even then, tear them into small pieces. The tendrils of Virginia Creeper are loaded with vitamin C, and are a delightful addition to salads.

Wild Grape
Vitis spp.

Most people have eaten grape leaves wrapped around a rice mixture as a filling. These are best prepared and used when young. The very young leaves of wild grape are sour and make an interesting addition to a salad or change the taste of a mix of pot greens. A little goes a long way, tear them into small pieces and only use a few leaves for each salad. Once the leaves are mature they are too tough to eat, and the tannins make them unpalatable. The tendrils of grape are loaded with vitamin C, and are a delightful addition to salads.

Wild Carrot
Daucus carota

This is another treat. It is a biennial, and in the second year is called Queen Anne's Lace. The root can be cooked like carrot (although it is tiny by comparison to our cultivated carrots). The root will be good throughout the plants first year, and the spring of the second year. After that, it is woody and quickly loses its taste. The first year leaves are a pleasant addition to a salad. The early leaves can be mistaken for wild hemlock, a poisonous plant, so proper identification is essential. Beginners should certainly have experienced help with this one. The bruised wild carrot will smell like carrot, hemlock does not.

Wood Sorrel and Sheep Sorrel
Oxalis montana and Rumex acetosella

This weed is familiar to many as it has a biting, citrusy sour taste from thin pale green leaves. All parts of this plant are edible, and as its taste gives away, it contains vitamin C. It adds a nice zing to salads, or even sandwiches. It has been used as a sort of tea as well, sweetened with honey. As the name implies, the wood does contain oxalic acid that can interfere with calcium absorption, so it should be used as a small addition rather than a main course. Both sorrels make a delicate and tasty spring soup, cooked with a few spring onions.

Yellow Dock
Rumex Crispus

Also known as curly dock. This weed is less commonly known but is one of my favorites. The name describes the yellow root, which is used as a tincture for iron deficiency. The leaves are clearly high in iron and calcium and noticeable for their chalky taste and iron-rich "mouth feel." Pesto made from yellow dock leaves is easy to make, lacks the slightly strong aftertaste of basil pestos, freezes well, and would appear to offer a richer variety of nutrients.

Yellow dock leaves can also be torn up and added to stir fries, added as a nice textural ingredient in salads, and combined with pot greens. While it tastes great as the only green in pesto, you'll want to combine it with other greens if you are simply boiling them or using them in salad.

Be sure to use the NARROW LEAFED variety – the wide leafed yellow dock is awful-tasting. Yellow dock is easy to identify once it goes to seed, as the seeds are a rust color and the leaves start to have what looks like rust spots on them. The leaves are edible all season long, but the plant is so rich and good tasting the bugs in your garden will start to munch on it as well.

Identifying wild plants and weeds

The Latin names have been given to ensure proper identification, and make it easier to look up each plant for positive identification BEFORE you eat it. Learning one or two new plants a year is a reasonable pace, and allows you to focus on all of the benefits and cycles of each plant. It also makes it less likely that you will mistake a plant. Field guides are often available at used or discounted bookstores, with full color photos, for as little as $1-$5. If you are using a book for identification the good photos matter more than the text. Purchase a good quality guide as well so that you can be sure and learn the poisonous plants in your area before you do any harvesting of uncultivated plants - also known as wildcrafting.

Strange behavior redefined

Wildcrafting and eating wild plants has gained some popularity, and even gourmet status. In many countries it is still the norm, and an important part of survival. It wasn't that long ago (within 100 years) that knowledge of wild food was valued and a part of everyday life. With industrialization, more and more city living, and status consciousness, wild food fell out of favor. Even today, people will tend to look askance at someone who encourages dandelions in their lawn and doesn't fight against weeds with chemicals and hoes. If I serve weeds to my dinner guests, I'm met with some skepticism, the first time, only later to become enthusiasm and gusto. Little by little, I'm seen as less and less strange.

More people are realizing that poisoning their lawns to be rid of weeds is not healthy for our environment, our families, our pets, or even the lawn itself! We need a fundamental shift in consciousness about the abundance of these "pest" plants. Where once they were sought after, many people consider it a failing to have any of these weeds in their lawns. Their fall from favor is perpetuated by those who label these nutrient rich plants as "pests" and sell products and services to eliminate them. Fear of weeds, and compulsive attempts to eliminate these valuable (and good tasting) plants, is the truly strange behavior.

There is a more intelligent, reasonable, resourceful, responsible, environmentally sound and even fun way to deal with these plants. Eat them!

The Recipes

Design - making things simple.

When it is time to choose a recipe, you'll need some basic information. How many will it serve? How long will it take? Are there any unusual ingredients or do you have the ingredients on hand? Is it a main dish or a side dish? Is any special equipment required? Does it make good leftovers? All of that information will be in the box on the upper right corner of the first page of each recipe.

> Serves:
> Time:
> Type of dish:
> Equipment:
> Leftovers:
> Ingredients:

The times given are an estimate. You may be faster or slower. Use time as a reference, but not as an absolute.

Many recipes have a "story" box as well. Food is special when it has a story. Have you ever served a special dish, and found yourself telling a tale while you eat? Do memories of your childhood or special occasions come back to you when you eat certain foods? The experience of taste and smell trigger powerful

> The Story:

memories and associations.

Before packaged food became such a common experience, most food had stories. The story may be where the recipe came from, experiences making it, how other people reacted to it, or what it reminds us of. It may include events or people important to us. The story is there to add dimension to the recipe, and to make these recipes less abstract.

I prefer recipes that are narrative, so that you don't have to glance at an ingredient list for the amount, and back to the text for what to do with it. The ingredient list is in the initial box, and then the ingredients including amounts are part of the recipe narrative.

Many of these recipes have variations, and I encourage you to improvise. Ideas for changes are found at the end of the recipe in italics. For some recipes, there is expanded information for the beginning cooks that more experienced cooks may want to skip over. We all started somewhere - wondering how to cook rice, how to use a steamer. So even if you are a true novice in the kitchen, you'll be O.K.

Measuring

All measurements are given in US terms. Capitol "T" means tablespoon, small "t" is teaspoon.

Greens are difficult to measure. Luckily it rarely matters that you have a precise amount. Most frozen greens come in 10 oz. boxes, so that is our standard. A 10 oz. box of frozen greens is equivalent of about 2 cups cooked greens. Fresh Collards, kale, chard, spinach etc. are most often sold as a "bunch". A bunch of greens is roughly equivalent to the 10 oz. frozen box. Greens reduce in size rather dramatically when cooked for even a few moments How much depends on the greens, but reducing by 1/2 or more is normal.

Of course, a poor bunch of greens quickly decreases in measure if there are many leaves to discard, or if it is all stems. If that is the case, you'll need to add more greens or adjust the recipe accordingly - but most are pretty forgiving.

If you are picking the greens, or freezing at home, you'll need to judge the amount that is equal to the store bought bunches, or the amount of cups of your frozen greens. A bunch is about a quart of greens with whole leaves, and not compacted. The weight will be right around a pound. The exact amount will vary depending on the type and size of the greens.

The amounts given for spices can be easily adjusted for individual taste. The amount of oil and butter is also minimized, you may want to add more.

The need for salt will vary greatly depending on what you're used to, so in most cases salt is not a part of the recipe, but something to be added at the table. In baking, salt is more important to add before baking, so that is the exception. You may especially find the soups to be very salt free. The mineral rich greens suffice for many people, and no added salt is required.

Pot Greens

Although the term "pot green" doesn't have a specific definition, it is commonly used to describe greens that are simply cooked, using a pot. Greens are used singularly, or in combinations. The combinations might be a matter of convenience (what is available or left over) or to blend or modify flavors.

If mustard is too hot by itself, it may be perfect combined with a bit of collards or chard to ease its bite. Sorrel cooked alone is much too sour for most people, but as a contributing flavor with kale it is just right. Similarly, bitter greens are often combined with bland to temper their taste. Wild greens and conventional greens can also be combined for new flavors.

Boiling greens in a pot is a traditional way to cook greens, often with the addition of lard or other fats. In this section, the definition is extended to include steamed, braised, sauted and boiled greens.

Cooking pot greens is as easy as it gets, other than eating them raw. But day after day this can get dull. These recipes rely on sauces, additions, and spices to make pot greens tasty, unusual, and varied.

Boiling

Serves: 2-4
Time: 10-40 minutes
Type of dish: side
Equipment: basic
Leftovers: keeps up to 3 days,
    freezes well
Ingredients: 1 bunch any greens or
    1 package frozen

The traditional way to cook pot greens is in a medium sized saucepan.

Start heating about 1 to 1 1/2 cups water in the saucepan. Wash and sort through the greens (skip this step for frozen greens). Remove some or all of the midrib, depending on greens and how they will be used.

Do not dry.

Cut or tear the greens into bite sized pieces and dd the greens, to the saucepan. Simmer on medium to low heat, covered, for 10-40 minutes, depending on the type of greens and how they will be used. Add more water if needed.

After you remove the greens, save the water for soups, or drink as a nutrient rich beverage hot or cold.

The most common pot green recipe may be Southern style collards, boiled with pork fat or bacon. I prefer to substitute olive oil which gives a lighter flavor, and is better for you.
Especially in the south, a variety of spring greens were used as pot greens including Poke, which is only safe to eat in the spring. The spring harvest for pot greens was much anticipated, coming as soon as February in many locations.
There is tradition and folk lore in the types of greens used and many are cherished for their spring tonic effect. Pot greens are also welcome year round, but nothing compares to the first fresh greens of early spring.

Steaming

Serves: 2-4
Time: 10-30 minutes
Type of dish: side
Equipment: steamer
Leftovers: keeps up to 3 days
    refrigerated, freezes well
Ingredients: 1 bunch any greens
    or 1 package frozen

Place a vegetable steamer in a saucepan with a tight fitting lid. Add enough water so that it covers the legs, but doesn't quite reach the bottom of the steamer basket.

Bring that to a boil while you wash the greens, remove all or part of the midrib and tear or chop the greens into bite sized pieces. Omit these steps if using frozen greens.

Add the greens to the basket, pressing down to fit, and cover. Steam for 10-40 minutes depending on greens used, and how they will be used.

A metal collapsible steamer basket is ideal. You can also use a bamboo steamer, placed over a wok with water below. This arrangement tends to take longer, with more steam able to escape. The advantage is you can stack them, you can steam more greens at once, and can put tougher greens in lower baskets, and more delicate above where it will be cooler. But plan to at least double the cooking time (and the amount of water used).

Sauteing

Serves: 2-4
Time: 3-20 minutes
Type of dish: side
Equipment: basic
Leftovers: keeps up to 3 days
    refrigerated, freezes well
Ingredients: 1 bunch any greens or
    1 package frozen, olive oil
    (water, vinegar, wine, and
    broth can also be used)

Wash, sort, and remove all or part of the midrib on one bunch greens. Tear or chop into bite sized pieces. Omit this step if using frozen greens.

Heat 2 T olive oil in a medium sized skillet on medium to medium high heat. Add greens. Stir carefully, they will reduce in size in a few moments, giving room to stir more thoroughly.

Cook 3-20 minutes, depending on greens and how they will be used. By using medium to medium high heat the greens cook quickly, but must be stirred nearly constantly at the beginning, and every minute or two once they have reduced in size.

Greens can be sauted in oil, butter, water, broth, wine, or vinegar. Each form has its own flavor. If you choose oil or butter, garlic and onion are often sauted first and the greens added after they are soft. Spices, chilies, and herbs can also cooked briefly before the greens are added.

If you are using water, broth, wine or vinegar, use 1/4 cup in place of oil. Add more water or broth as needed. Adding more vinegar or wine might overpower the greens and is not advised.

Braising

Braising combines the previous methods. Braising refers to using a bit of fat and a bit of moisture, cooking more slowly, and using a cover. Braising tends to infuse the greens with more flavor, especially if the liquid is a bit of wine, vinegar, broth, or water to which spices have been added.

There are many variations.

You can start with the oil and add the liquid gradually.

You can start with the liquid and add fat towards the end.

You can use the water clinging to the greens as the only moisture.

You can add a dash of wine or vinegar as you add the greens to the heated oil.

Which ever method you choose, turn the heat to low, stir occasionally, add more liquid if needed (don't overdo it – add a small amount each time), and keep covered. This method will take 20-40 minutes depending on the greens used.

Simple Braised Greens

Wash, sort, and remove all or part of the midrib on one bunch greens. Tear or chop into bite sized pieces. Omit this step if using frozen greens. Do not dry. Chop or tear into bite sized pieces.

Serves: 2
Time: 20-40 minutes
Type of dish: side
Equipment: skillet with lid
Leftovers: keeps up to 3 days refrigerated, freezes well
Ingredients: 1 bunch any greens or 1 package frozen, olive oil, liquid (wine, broth, water, vinegar)

Thinly slice a small onion. Heat 2 T olive oil in a medium sized skillet. Add onion to oil, cook on medium heat until onion is soft and fragrant. Add greens.

Sprinkle greens with 2 T vinegar (balsamic is a good choice). Cover and reduce heat to low. Stir every few minutes, add a little water if needed. Cook until greens are very wilted, and softened, 10-30 minutes, depending on the greens used.

Garlic Braised Greens

Serves: 2
Time: 20-40 minutes
Type of dish: side
Equipment: garlic press is helpful,
   skillet with lid
Leftovers: keeps up to 3 days
   refrigerated, freezes well
Ingredients: 1 bunch any greens or
   1 package frozen, olive oil,
   garlic, vegetable broth

Wash and sort through 1 bunch any greens, or combination. Do not dry the leaves. Cut or tear into bite sized pieces. If using frozen greens, omit washing and cutting steps.

Heat 2 T olive oil on medium heat in a medium sized skillet. Add 4 cloves garlic, minced or pressed Stir the garlic as it cooks, for about 1 minute.

Add the greens to the skillet, and stir until wilted and reduced in size. Add 1 cup vegetable broth. Use prepared broth, home made broth, vegetable bouillon cubes reconstituted with hot water, or other liquid you may have.

Cover, and simmer on low heat for about 20 -30 minutes, depending on the greens used, stirring a few times.

Vinegar Braised Greens

Heat 2 T olive oil in a medium sized skillet. Thinly slice 1 medium onion. Cook in oil on medium high heat for about 2 minutes, until onion is soft.

Wash and then chop into bite sized pieces 1 bunch greens, or use 1 package frozen greens. This recipe is especially good for collards and kale, and wild greens such as amaranth.

Serves: 2
Time: 30-40 minutes to cook, 5 minutes to prepare
Type of dish: side
Equipment: skillet with lid
Leftovers: keeps up to 3 days refrigerated, freezes well
Ingredients: 1 bunch any greens or 1 package frozen, olive oil, onion, balsamic or other vinegar

Add greens to skillet, and stir. Reduce heat to low. Pour 1/4 cup of balsamic vinegar over the greens, and 1/4 cup of water. Cover with a lid.

Cook over low heat, stirring occasionally, for 30-40 minutes, depending on greens. Add more water if needed to avoid sticking.

You can also use other vinegars instead of balsamic including fruit vinegars, herbal vinegars, homemade shitaki mushroom vinegar, white wine, etc.

Wine Braised Greens

Serves: 2
Time: 20-40 minutes
Type of dish: side
Equipment: skillet with lid
Leftovers: keeps up to 3 days
    refrigerated, freezes well
Ingredients: 1 bunch any greens or
    1 package frozen, olive oil,
    liquid (wine, broth, water,
    vinegar)

Wash and sort through 1 bunch tender greens: spinach, bok choy, lambs quarters, mache, and chard are all good choices. Brussel sprouts are particularly tasty split in half and cooked this way.

Do not dry after washing the greens. Chop into bite sized pieces. If using frozen greens, omit washing and cutting.

In a medium sized skillet, over medium low heat saute a small onion, very thinly sliced (as thin as you can manage) in 1/4 cup dry white wine.

When the onion is soft, about 2-3 minutes, add greens, cover, and cook on low until wilted, and the liquid is absorbed, about 10 - 30 minutes depending on the greens used.

Serve with balsamic or other vinegar on the side.

When are they done?

No matter the method you use, the greens are cooked lightly when they turn a brighter green are reduced in size, and become soft. This may take just a few minutes, and is sufficient for many recipes. You may want to lengthen the cooking time, so that stems and stalks are also palatable, 20 minutes or more.

How long to cook the greens is really a matter of preference. Overcooked is never good, when the greens are disintegrating and form a blobby mass. They should still have their individual integrity and shape. For some recipes the lightest cooking, followed by a cold water plunge, is ideal. Most pot greens are cooked about 20 minutes, longer if there is a large amount, and if the greens are older or tougher, or if you want very soft melt in your mouth greens.

How do you serve them?

Pot greens can be eaten as is, with a bit of olive oil drizzled over them, with a dash of parmesan cheese, a sprinkle of balsamic or other vinegar, with more elaborate sauces and additions, or integrated into other recipes.

Pot greens can also be served over rice, millet, buckwheat, or other whole grains. They can be served with pasta, or simply wrapped in a tortilla or with a sheet of nori seaweed.

The next few pages have some simple recipes, followed by more elaborate ideas.

Hot Peppers and Greens

Serves: 4
Time: 10 minutes prep, 20-40
        minutes to cook
Type of dish: side
Equipment: garlic press and spice
        grinder are helpful
Leftovers: freezes easily, makes
        good leftovers hot or cold
Ingredients: 2 bunches any greens
        or 2 packages frozen, olive oil,
        garlic, dried hot pepper

Wash and tear or cut into bite sized pieces 2 bunches kale, collards, spinach, chard, other greens, or a combination of these. If using frozen greens, just proceed to next step.

Steam or saute until lightly cooked. Set aside.

In 2 T olive oil, and medium high heat saute 2 cloves garlic, finely minced or pressed in a garlic press, and 1/2 dried hot pepper, minced fine, or put through a spice grinder. Depending on heat desired, you can use jalapeno, habenero, chipote, or others. Increase amount of pepper if desired.

When you first start to smell the garlic, as it slightly browns, add the cooked greens. Stir quickly over medium heat for about a minute.

Prepare the hot pepper mixture, but do not cook the greens in advance. Wash the greens, but leave them wet. When the recipe says to add greens, add the wet raw greens. Cover and let cook over low heat for 20-30 minutes, stirring occasionally. Add more water as needed to prevent sticking.

Greens with Cheese Sauce

Prepare 2 bunches or 2 packages frozen any type of green by steaming, boiling, or sauteing.

Make a roux. This is done by melting 4 T butter in a sauce pan, then adding 3 T whole wheat flour. Stir so the flour will cook in the butter, about a minute. Using a small whisk to stir is the best tool.

When flour is cooked, slowly add 2 cups of milk or milk substitute. Soy milk, rice milk, and cows milk all work well. Over medium high heat, stir constantly with the whisk as the mixture thickens, about 3-5 minutes. Do not let it boil, but a few bubbles are O.K.

> Serves: 4
> Time: 20-40 minutes for the greens to cook, 10 minutes to make the sauce
> Type of dish: side
> Equipment: a whisk helps
> Leftovers: Once mixed with the greens, the sauce will not reheat very well.
> Ingredients: 2 bunches any greens or 2 packages frozen, butter, 3 T whole wheat flour, 2 cups milk (or milk substitute), cheese, tamari

When the mixture thickens add 1 cup grated cheese, or a non-dairy cheese that melts well. Medium or sharp cheddar work well, the milder jack cheese is also a fine choice. Stir well, as the cheese melts. It will be a thick gooey sauce. Add a splash of tamari if desired.

Pour over cooked greens.

You can leave out the cheese, add some fresh herbs (cilantro or dill are good choices) and just use the cream sauce over the greens.

Using whole wheat flour in your roux gives it a nuttier flavor, and slightly courser texture. Making a thickened sauce may seem complex to a new cook, but really couldn't be simpler. If the sauce fails to thicken, adding cheese is a remedy.

A basic cheese sauce can be use over vegetables, grains, and to make your own macaroni and cheese.

Garlic Treat Greens

Serves: 4
Time: 20-40 minutes to cook greens, 5 minutes to prepare garlic
Type of dish: side
Equipment: a garlic press helps
Leftovers: will reheat well, can be frozen
Ingredients: 2 bunches greens or 2 packages frozen, garlic, olive oil

Steam or boil 2 bunches greens, washed and cut or torn into bite sized pieces. If you are using frozen greens, omit washing and tearing.

Meanwhile, saute 4 cloves garlic minced or pressed in 2 T olive oil until just beginning to brown and stick to the pan. Add cooked greens, stir together, turn off heat and cover, let sit for 3-4 minutes.

Horseradish Sauce and Greens

Serves: 4
Time: 20-40 minutes to cook greens, 5 minutes to prepare sauce
Type of dish: side
Equipment: none
Leftovers: doesn't keep well
Ingredients: 2 bunches milder greens or 2 packages frozen, 1/4 cup light cream, prepared horseradish

Steam or boil 2 bunches greens, washed and cut or torn into bite sized pieces. For best results, use milder greens, mustard and bitter greens will tend to clash with the horseradish taste. If you are using frozen greens, omit washing and tearing.

When the greens are almost ready whisk together 1/4 c light cream with 2 T Prepared horseradish. Pour over cooked greens

Sesame Seed Dressing

Serves: 4
Time: 20-40 minutes to
   cook greens, 5 minutes
   to make sauce
Type of dish: side
Equipment: cast iron skillet
   works best
Leftovers: reheats well
Ingredients: 2 bunches
   greens or 2 packages
   frozen, sesame seeds,
   olive or sesame oil,
   lemon juice, vinegar,
   honey, garlic, tamari
   (or salt).

Steam or boil 2 bunches greens, washed and cut or torn into bite sized pieces. If you are using frozen greens, omit washing and tearing.

Dry roast 2 T sesame seeds in heavy skillet over high heat until slightly browned – about a minute. Let cool.

Combine in a jar with lid 1/3 cup olive oil (or use sesame oil), 1 T lemon juice, 1 T vinegar, a scant T honey, a clove of garlic minced or pressed, and 1/4 t salt or tamari. Shake well.

Serve over warm greens.

Greens with Feta and Pine Nuts

Serves: 4
Time: 20-40 minutes to
   cook greens, 2 minutes
   to combine
Type of dish: side
Equipment: basic
Leftovers: not advised
Ingredients: 2 bunches
   milder greens or 2
   packages frozen, 1/2
   cup feta cheese, 1/4 cup
   pine nuts.

Steam or boil 2 bunches greens, washed and cut or torn into bite sized pieces. If you are using frozen greens, omit washing and tearing.

Crumble about 1/2 cup feta cheese and add to hot greens with about 1/4 cup pine nuts (raw or dry roasted).

The feta cheese is important to this recipe because of the strong flavor and also for the salty taste.

Nutty greens

Steam or boil 2 bunches greens, washed and cut or torn into bite sized pieces. Or use two packages frozen greens, and omit washing and cutting.

While they are cooking dry roast 1 cup of chopped nuts. In order of preference, I like pine nuts, walnuts, pecans, hazelnuts, cashews, sunflower seeds, peanuts. You can also combine some of these for a more exotic taste.

Serves: 4
Time: 20-30 minutes for greens to cook, 10-15 to prepare the nut sauce
Type of dish: side or possible light main dish
Equipment: food processor
Leftovers: reheats well, do not freeze
Ingredients: 2 bunches or two packages frozen greens, 1 cup nuts (see list), feta cheese, vinegar

Dry roasting requires a heavy bottomed skillet, cast iron is perfect. The skillet is heated, nuts are added with no fat or liquid. You must stir constantly, and use a fairly high heat. Most nuts need only about 1-3 minutes to roast nicely and bring out their flavor.

Let the nuts cool slightly but while still warm place into a food processor. Add 6 oz. crumbled feta cheese. Pulse them lightly, until they are slightly chopped, and feta is distributed. Add 1 T vinegar (balsamic, red wine, or herbal) and 1 T water. Pulse once or twice just to distribute the liquid.

Mix with warm greens and serve.

Simple Miso Sauce

Steam or boil 2 bunches greens, washed and cut or torn into bite sized pieces. Or use two packages frozen greens, and omit washing and cutting.

Mix together 1/4 cup warm water, 2 T of a dark rich miso, a splash of lemon juice, and stir over warm cooked greens.

Citrus Miso Sauce

Steam or boil 2 bunches greens, washed and cut or torn into bite sized pieces. Or use two packages frozen greens, and omit washing and cutting.

Mix together 2 T lemon juice, 2 T orange juice, 1 T olive oil, 1/2 T light vinegar, 2 T miso and stir over warm cooked greens.

Sesame Miso Sauce

Steam or boil 2 bunches greens, washed and cut or torn into bite sized pieces. Or use two packages frozen greens, and omit washing and cutting.

Mix together 1 T sesame oil, 2 T miso, 2 T lemon juice, 1 T crushed sesame seeds, 2 T light vinegar (wine or rice), 2 cloves minced or crushed garlic, 1/2 cup water, 2 T fresh herbs such as tarragon, basil, oregano, or cilantro.

Stir over warm cooked greens.

Serves: 4
Time: 10 minutes to
*   prepare sauce*
Type of dish: side
Equipment: basic
Leftovers: use within 2-3
*   days*
Ingredients: 2 bunches
*   greens or 2 packages*
*   frozen, sesame oil,*
*   miso, lemon juice,*
*   sesame seeds, wine or*
*   rice vinegar, garlic,*
*   tarragon, basil,*
*   oregano, cilantro*

Vinegar Miso Sauce

Steam or boil 2 bunches greens, washed and cut or torn into bite sized pieces. Or use two packages frozen greens, and omit washing and cutting.

Bring to a boil in a small sauce pan 1/2 cup water, 1/3 cup vinegar. Remove from heat, and add 1 T miso.

In the same pan or a sauce pan, heat 2 T olive oil and saute 1/2 onion, minced and chopped. Add 1/4 t basil, oregano, and tarragon (optional).

Serves: 4
Time: 20-40 minutes to
*   cook greens, 10*
*   minutes for sauce*
Type of dish: side
Equipment: basic
Leftovers: reheats well, use
*   within one day*
Ingredients: 2 bunches or 2
*   packages frozen greens,*
*   miso, vinegar, olive oil,*
*   onion, optional herbs*

Add to the miso vinegar water mixture and stir well. Stir over warm cooked greens.

Simple Greens With Miso Vinegar

Serves: 2
Time: 20-40 minutes to
       cook greens, 2 minutes
       for sauce
Type of dish: side
Equipment: basic
Leftovers: reheats well, but
       use within a day
Ingredients: 1 bunches or 1
       packages frozen greens,
       miso, white wine
       vinegar, honey

Steam or boil 2 bunches greens, washed and cut or torn into bite sized pieces. Or use two packages frozen greens, and omit washing and cutting.

While the greens are cooking,combine and mix well together 2 T miso with 2 T water and 1 T white wine vinegar. Adjust to taste, adding more vinegar if desired, and a drop or two of honey.

This is easily mixed by shaking in a small jar. Add to greens, and stir well. Serve warm.

Miso provides a deep, salty, full taste to foods. It is a fermented product, and comes in many forms and colors. Which miso to use is a matter of taste, I like the deep dark rich somewhat chunky types. A little goes a long way. It lasts in the refrigerator for many months.
Always add miso at the end of the cooking process, and do not boil, as heating destroys the rich enzymes and good bacteria that miso provides.

Simple Polenta with Greens

Serves: 4
Time: 20-40 minutes to cook greens, 25 minutes to cook polenta and garlic and combine ingredients
Type of dish: side or main
Equipment: a whisk will help
Leftovers: use within 2-3 days
Ingredients: 2 bunches or 2 packages frozen greens, 1 cup cornmeal, garlic, optional onion, optional olives

Steam or boil 2 bunches greens, chopped into smaller than bite sized pieces. Most any green will work well in this recipe, so it is a matter of taste.

Chop the greens pretty fine before or after they are cooked. Before will be easier. If you are using frozen greens, let them thaw, chop even finer, and use plain water for the next step.

Save the water from steaming or boiling the greens, pour it into a medium sized sauce pan, and add more water so that you have about 5 cups. Add or subtract from this if you want thinner or thicker polenta.

Bring the water to a boil and slowly add 1 cup of cornmeal, stirring frequently and very thoroughly. Once the cornmeal mixed in stir constantly and thoroughly, frequently scraping down the sides and bottom of the pan.

Using a wooden spoon is traditional, and just seems like the right fit. A few bubbles are O.K., but do not let it boil. It will thicken in 2-3 minutes. Reduce the heat, keep stirring, but it doesn't have to be as constant.

In a separate skillet, saute   2 cloves of garlic in 2 T olive oilOptional – add thinly sliced white onion. You may also choose to add some coarsely chopped black olives.

When onions and garlic are soft, add to the cornmeal polenta with the cooked chopped greens. Cook on low heat for another 10 to 15 minutes. The result should be creamy, and thick.

Serve in bowls. Garnish with more olives if desired.

Sun dried tomatoes make a tasty addition as well as fresh basil.

For truly fabulous polenta, the only option is to use fresh stone ground corn meal. The taste is very different and so much better than what you buy in the store. Not only is it fresh and nutty tasting, but the stone ground method creates a flour that isn't as dry and powdery as other milling methods.

When you grind it yourself, you can also choose how fine you want the flour to be. If you are serious about baking with whole grains, or even just about polenta, a small grinder is easily obtained.

For the last 20 plus years, I have used a Little Ark made by the Retsel Corporation. (www.retsel.com) While I started out always grinding by hand, it was converted to electrical power many years ago. This made it easier to grind the 20 cups of flour I needed for baking bread.

My polenta, cornbread, and other baked goods always elicit positive comments and requests for the recipes -- and I have to explain that it is the fresh ground flour that makes it taste so good, not the recipe itself.

In Latin America, you can still find local mills that grind corn on the spot.

Cold Korean Style Greens

Steam or boil 1 bunch greens, washed and cut or torn into bite sized pieces. Or use 1 package frozen greens and omit washing and chopping. Kale, collards, spinach and chard are good choices.

Plunge cooked greens into cold water. Drain well, and also pat dry with a towel.

Mix together 2 t tamari sauce, 1/2 t honey, 1 t crushed sesame seeds, 1 T sesame oil, 1 T minced onion or scallion, 1 t red or white wine vinegar, salt to taste

> Serves: 2
> Time::10-30 minutes for greens to cook, 5 minutes to prepure dressing
> Type of dish: side
> Equipment: mortar and pestle to crush sesame seeds is helpful
> Leftovers: would reheat well, but do not freeze
> Ingredients: 1 bunch greens or 1 package frozen, tamari, honey, sesame seeds, sesame oil, onion or scallion, red or white wine vinegar

Pour the dressing over the cold greens. Let sit refrigerated for 1-3 hours before serving.

For a slightly different taste you could add 1/4 t chili oil (more or less to taste) to the dressing mix, dry roast the sesame seeds before crushing or add 1 t finely grated fresh ginger to dressing

Greek Style Garlic Yogurt

Serves: 4
Time: 10 minutes to
    assemble, 1 hour to
    set in the
    refrigerator, 1-2
    hours to strain the
    yogurt
Type of dish: sauce
Equipment: you will need
    cheesecloth
Leftovers: The sauce will
    keep in the
    refrigerator for up to
    a week. Once it is
    combined with
    greens, use it right
    away.
Ingredients: Yogurt,
    cucumber, garlic,
    olive oil, dill
    weed,salt, 2 bunches
    or 2 packages frozen
    greens (kale, collards,
    spinach, almost any
    other pot green)

For best results, strain 4 cups yogurt by placing it in a cheesecloth, tie it into a bundle, and let it drip for a few hours until it is more solid. You can omit this step, but the sauce will be drippy and not as nice a texture. See next page for a recipe to make home made yogurt.

Mix strained yogurt with a small size cucumber, very finely chopped. Traditionally the skin and seeds are removed, if the skin isn't bitter and the seeds are small I don't bother. You could grate the cucumber, but then you have to press the excess water out of it, losing some of the nutrition and taste.

Add 2-4 cloves garlic, pressed or very finely minced. Some people like even more garlic. Stir in 1 T good quality olive oil, 1/4 t dill weed (optional), a pinch of salt. Mix thoroughly and let stand in the refrigerator for at least one hour.

Steam or boil 2 bunches greens, washed and cut or torn into bite sized pieces. Serve with yogurt on the side.

This is also good with the greens and yogurt served over grains, including rice, millet, and quinoa.

This is a also a wonderful sauce for sandwiches, as a vegetable dip, as a sauce for a vegetable bake, and over just grains.

Choose a yogurt with active cultures, or make your own using the recipe from the next page.

Homemade Yogurt

Serves: enough for 1-2 weeks
Time: 15 minutes to heat and make, 3-12 hours to sit
Type of dish: versatile ingredient
Equipment: thermometer, wooden spoon, large glass or enamel pot
Leftovers: make enough to last a while
Ingredients: 1 gallon milk, 1 cup yogurt

In a large glass or enamel pot, heat one gallon of high quality milk to 118 degrees. Turn off heat. Stir in 1 cup fairly fresh yogurt that contains quality live cultures.

Place in yogurt maker, or pour into thick glass jars and place in insulated place, place in oven that is about 100 degrees. or near a light bulb. Culture for at least 3-5 hours, or even overnight. The longer it is cultured the more tart.

Store in the refrigerator in glass jars for up to two weeks. Ideally, make it once a week saving some from the last batch for the new.

It is best to use glass with every step including the thermometer, and use a wooden spoon to stir.

The glass jars with the hinged lid and rubber gasket are perfect for making the yogurt, and storing it in the refrigerator. They are thick enough to hold the heat, don't have a metal lid, and easy to handle when you want to use the yogurt.

To make less, just reduce the recipe by half or more.

Making your own yogurt is a really simple and satisfying experience.

Greens with Almonds and Ginger

Serves: 2
Time: 20-40 minutes to
    cook greens, 5 minutes
    to make sauce
Type of dish: side
Equipment: basic, cast iron
    skillet helps
Leftovers: will reheat, use
    within a day.
Ingredients: 1 bunch fresh
    or 1 package frozen
    greens, almonds,
    sesame oil, fresh (or
    frozen) ginger root

Steam or boil 1 bunch greens, washed and cut or torn into bite sized pieces. Or use 1 package frozen greens and omit washing and tearing.

While the greens are cooking dry roast 1/4 cup of almonds, chopped. To dry roast almonds, a cast iron skillet is preferred. Stir on high heat in a dry skillet, about 2-3 minutes, until lightly browned. Add nuts to cooked greens.

With the skillet still hot, add 2 T sesame oil. Add about 2 inches of fresh ginger root, peeled and sliced thin, then diced.

Saute on medium heat until fragrant and just turning light brown, stirring constantly. Add to greens.

Ginger root can be frozen, as is, and easily peeled and chopped without thawing. I don't even put it in a container and it keeps fine for months.

Peanut Sauce

Steam or boil 2 bunches greens, washed and cut or torn into bite sized pieces. Or use two packages frozen greens, and omit washing and cutting.

While they are cooking heat 2 T olive oil in a medium skillet. On medium high heat add 2 garlic cloves, minced or pressed

Let the garlic cook (about 1 minute) and then add 1 t crushed and minced or powdered red pepper (add more or less to taste) followed by 6 T peanut butter, 1/2 t honey.

Slowly stir in 1 cup milk , (soy milk, or almond milk may be used) and 1 t lemon juice.

Cook slowly on low heat, stirring often, about 5 minutes, or until it thickens slightly. Add 1/2 water, more or less, as needed so it is not too thick.

Combine with greens, and serve warm.

Serves: 4
Time: 20-40 minutes to cook greens, 10-15 minutes to cook sauce
Type of dish: side or part of a main dish
Equipment: a whisk is helpful
Leftovers: keeps 2-3 days before combining with greens, use right away once it has been mixed with the greens.
Ingredients: 2 bunches fresh or 2 packages frozen greens, olive oil, garlic, red pepper, peanut butter, honey, milk or milk substitute, lemon juice

This is especially good when served with greens and cooked pasta, greens and a grain such as brown rice, or in combination with other vegetables.

Pureed Greens

Serves: 2-4
Time: 20 minutes
Type of dish: sauce
Equipment: food processor
    or blender
Leftovers: freezes well,
    keeps at least 3 days in
    the refrigerator
Ingredients: 1 bunch fresh
    or 1 package frozen
    greens; optional: onion,
    garlic, pine nuts or
    walnuts, tahini, olive
    oil, vinegar

Using either 1/4 cup water or 2 T olive oil, saute one bunch or one package greens such as kale, collards, spinach, mustards, or similar green. You can use large leaves ripped small enough to easily stir. Remove most or all of the mid rib.

Cook just enough that they are bright green and softened. This could take 5-15 minutes, depending on the greens used. If using frozen greens, cook until heated.

Remove from heat, cool slightly and place in food processor or blender with just enough water to be able to puree into a smooth sauce.

This sauce can be used over rice, pasta, baked potatoes, steamed vegetables, as a spread on bread or rice cakes, and as a vegetable dip.

Kids often enjoy dips more than vegetables. When the dip is the vegetable there is no problem with overdoing the dip and leaving the vegetables.

For additional flavor any of these variations can be used.

Saute a small thinly sliced onion before adding greens to cook.

Add 1-2 cloves chopped raw garlic to food processor.

Add 1/2 cup pine nuts or walnuts to food processor.

Add 1/4 cup tahini to food processor.

If you didn't use olive oil to saute   , you can drizzle a bit into the food processor (1-2 T).

You can add 1 T balsamic vinegar, a splash of lemon juice, and a 1/4 to 1/2 t tamari to food processor.

Salads and Uncooked Greens

Salads are all about greens, and salads are no longer simply iceberg lettuce and a sugary bottled dressing. A salad is the perfect medium to experience the complexity of taste, texture, color, and pleasure that greens can impart.

Many of the dark green leafy vegetables are an acquired taste. The four primary flavors we seek are salt, sweet, sour and bitter. Of these, bitter may be the one we most avoid and are least accustomed to.

Bitter is a taste to get used to. Once you have, it is a pleasure for its complexity, its intensity, and it many variations. Of course not all greens are bitter, some are also sweet, salty, and sour.

Begin to eat fresh greens in the spring, when they are the most sweet. Continue through the summer, as the bitter element enters the leaves and slowly adds more flavor to the plant. Your tolerance and appreciation for bitterness will also increase.

This section begins with a salad brainstorm – describing nearly 70 possible ingredients that can be part of a salad. That beginning is followed by some specific recipes for salads that include greens.

Fresh Green Salads

A fresh, well prepared salad with a variety of textures, tastes, and colors is a wonderful addition to any meal, or a meal in itself. Here is how you can add dark green leafy vegetables to your salad, and enjoy the benefits of raw greens.

The key is to balance the presence of the darker greens, which tend to have a bitter taste, with the sweet greens and vegetables. Much of this is an acquired taste – while initially most people go easy on the more bitter raw greens, you should be able to slowly change the balance as your palate expands and adjusts to the new tastes.

The ingredients suggested below are in descriptive categories so that you can more easily guide the overall experience of your salad. Choose just a few from a couple groups, or indulge in a more complex salad with more than a dozen different ingredients. Keep it interesting, remember the value of color, and choose the ingredients you will enjoy. A "salad" doesn't have to be mostly lettuce.

Many people also think of a salad as containing all uncooked ingredients. You can steam some vegetables to add, you can even steam all or part of the greens. Conventional lettuce is not improved by steaming, but the hardier dark green leafy vegetables often are.

Potential Salad Ingredients:

Greens –

The bitter greens
Arugula
Endive
Radicchio

The earthier more substantial greens
Kale
Collards
Endive
Turnip greens
Beet greens

Sweeter and mild greens
    Spinach
    Swiss chard
    Chinese cabbage
    Mache
    Bok choy
    Rapini
    Conventional lettuces

Sour greens
    Sorrel
    Wood or sheep sorrel
    New young leaves Virginia creeper
    New young leaves Wild Grape

Hot or tangy greens
    Mustard
    Watercress

Wild greens
    Chickweed
    Dandelion
    Garlic Mustard
    Lamb's Quarters
    Plantain
    Purslane
    Wild Carrot leaves (and slivered root)
    Yellow dock
    Young red raspberry leaves

Fresh herbs for flavor (tear or chop into tiny pieces)
    Tarragon
    Oregano
    Cilantro
    Basil
    Chervil
    Borage
    Parsley
    Rosemary - crushed or rubbed
    Fennel

Other additions –

Crunchy and textural add-ins
  Sprouts – mung, sunflower, fenugreek, alfalfa, etc.
  Seaweed – dried dulse, dried kelp
  Green and red bell pepper chunks or slivers
  Cucumber (use an organic cucumber, don't peel it, take a fork
    and gouge the skin with the fork tines from top to bottom,
    all the way around. When sliced, the sides are a pretty green
    and white stripe effect)
  Raw summer squash (zucchini and yellow or crook neck) (slice
    at a 45 degree angle, rotate the squash 1/4 turn, slice at same
    angle, keep rotating and slicing – you'll end up with wedges
    rather than slices which hold together better and have more
    interesting texture)
  Celery pieces
  Fennel root slices
  Jerusalem Artichoke (sunchoke) slices

Poignant additions
  Olives
  Banana pepper rounds
  Jalapeno slivers
  Wild grape or Virginia creeper vine tendrils
  Onions – white, red, leeks, scallions, sliced thin
  Garlic slivers
  Soaked raisins - 30 minutes in warm water or overnight
  Mallow fruit (cheeses)

Protein sources
  Garbanzo beans
  Sunflower seeds
  Pine nuts, walnuts, slivered almonds, (roast them for extra
  flavor)
  Grated Cheese – cheddar, feta,
  Hard boiled eggs

Fun and colorful ingredients
Flowers
  violet, dame's rocket, evening flowering lichness, nasturtium,
  pansy, day lilly, and more

Pickled things
   Cucumber
   Beet
   Seaweed
   Kim chi

Vegetables raw
   Cauliflower
   Broccoli
   Asparagus
   Fresh peas and beans
   Avocado slices
   Dulse, a type of seaweed
   Beets
   Grated carrot
   Thinly shredded red cabbage (or grated)
   Mushrooms - all types

Vegetables lightly steamed
   Asparagus
   Brussel sprouts
   Peas and beans

Turning a Green Salad into a Pasta Salad

Almost any pasta does well as a salad. The shapes are fun, including elbows, shells, spirals, and more. You can also use regular spaghetti, angel hair and linguine. Whole wheat pasta doesn't do well cold, however. I use artichoke flour, semolina, spinach, buckwheat (soba) and other fancy pastas. Cook just to tender, do not overcook or it may be slimy in the salad. Rinse with cold water.

When pasta is the foundation of the salad, decrease the greens, use lots of fresh vegetables, and otherwise use the preceding list to choose what you'd enjoy. Use dressings that include oil. Mayonnaise based dressings are good with pasta, but not with the normal green salad. Mayonnaise with a bit of tamari, vinegar, and lemon juice is a simple dressing that will work for most pasta salads.

Once the salad is assembled, chill for at least an hour before serving so the flavors have a chance to blend.

Dressings

How you dress a salad will make all the difference. You may have favorite commercial salad dressings. You may enjoy a simple splash of oil and vinegar. Other dressings are easily made, and complement salads of both simple and multiple ingredients. Why not take five more minutes to make a fresh tasty dressing?

The following are a few of my favorites, and one manages to sneak greens into the dressing itself. A few of the dressings from the last chapter for cooked greens can also be used as salad dressings. Try the Yogurt Sauce, thinned with a bit of water, the dressing from Korean Style Cold Greens, any of the miso dressings, or the Sesame Seed Dressing.

Olive Oil and Vinegar

I buy a basic organic olive oil for cooking, and pay for premium olive oil to use for salad dressings and to sprinkle on other foods. It is worth the investment. I also keep on hand at least a dozen different vinegars, so there is a lot to choose from. Read more about vinegars on page 141.

> Serves: 1
> Time: less than a minute
> Type of dish: dressing
> Equipment: none
> Leftovers: none
> Ingredients: olive oil,
>   vinegar

The simplest salad dressing for an individual serving is 1 t good quality olive oil sprinkled on the salad followed by 1 t any vinegar. Adjust proportions to taste.

Basic Tahini Dressing

Serves: 4-6
Time: 5 minutes
Type of dish: dressing
Equipment: jar with lid
Leftovers: doesn't freeze,
    but keeps in the
    refrigerator for 3-5
    days
Ingredients: tamari, garlic,
    honey, olive oil,
    vinegar, tahini

In a pint jar combine 1/2 cup water, 1 T tamari, 1-3 cloves minced or pressed garlic (depending on your preference), 2 t honey, 1/3 cup olive oil, 1/4 cup vinegar, and 3 T tahini.

Shake well, and pour over salad.

The olive oil will cause this to be semi-solid when it is cold, spoon it onto your salad and as it warms up it will turn more liquid.

Wild Green Tahini Dressing

Serves: 4-6
Time: 10-15 minutes,
    including picking
    weeds
Type of dish: dressing
Equipment: blender, or food
    processor or blender
    stick
Leftovers: will keep
    refrigerated for 3-5
    days
Ingredients: raisins, wild
    greens, tamari, garlic,
    olive oil

Set about 1/8 of cup of raisins to soak in 1/2 cup warm water. While they are soaking, gather 10-15 dandelion leaves, or use 1/2 cup chickweed, or 10-15 small yellow dock leaves

You can use a blender, a food processor or a blender stick (also called a hand blender) to make this. I prefer the blender stick. In the food processor, blender, or in a jar that the blender stick will fit into combine 1 T tamari, 1-3 whole cloves garlic (depending on your preference), 1/3 cup olive oil, 1/4 cup vinegar, and 3 T tahini.

Blend, then add the greens and the rehydrated raisins. Blend until smooth, and the greens have been fully incorporated.

The olive oil will cause this to be semi-solid when it is cold, spoon it onto your salad and as it warms up it will turn more liquid.

Non Traditional Tabbouleh

Serves: 4-6
Time: 1 1/2 hours
        refrigeration needed,
        10 minutes to prepare
Type of dish: side
Equipment: basic
Leftovers: does not freeze,
        eat within 1-2 days
Ingredients: Bulgur or
        cracked wheat, 1 bunch
        fresh greens, fresh
        tomatoes, cucumber,
        parsley, scallions, olive
        oil, lemon juice

Prepare 2 cups bulgur wheat. Place bulgar in heat proof bowl. Add 4 cups boiling water, cover and let sit for 15 minutes. I use a stainless steel bowl and invert a plate over it. Refrigerate when all the water has been absorbed.

Very lightly steam a bunch of kale, collards, spinach, Swiss chard, (if you dare you could even use mustard greens). Do not use frozen greens. Remove them from the heat immediately as they turn a bright green, and plunge into cold water, or rinse with cold water. Press out water. Pat with a towel so that they are not dripping. Chop them into very small pieces, less than an inch in diameter. Put the greens into a medium sized mixing bowl.

Dice 3-4 fresh tomatoes. Canned will just not be the same, so don't try it. Add to greens. Dice a small cucumber. I include the seeds and peel, you may want to remove the seeds if they are large. With organic cucumbers the peel is rarely bitter, but taste a piece to make sure. Add this to the bowl.

Finely chop a half cup parsley and add to bowl (can be omitted). Finely chop 2-3 scallions, including most of the green. If not available use Vidalia onion, or thinly sliced red onion. Add this to the bowl.

Toss together the grain, the greens, and the vegetables. Add 4 T good quality olive oil, juice from two lemons (about 4 T if you use bottled juice)

Adjust these amounts to taste. Add a pinch of salt.

Refrigerate 1 hour to blend flavors and serve cold.

Quinoa Salad

Serves: 6
Time: 30 minutes to
     prepare, 3 hours to
     refrigerate
Type of dish: side or main
Equipment: basic
Leftovers: does not freeze,
     keeps in the
     refrigerator 1-2 days
Ingredients: quinoa, ume
     plum vinegar, fresh
     mild or hearty greens,
     sweet peppers,
     cucumber, cabbage
     cilantro and onion are
     suggested. Additional
     vegetables are optional.

The Quinoa must be carefully rinsed, it has a bitter taste if you don't rinse it really well. I use a fine strainer, and stir it with my fingers under the tap. Place in a sauce pan, 2 cups Quinoa with 4 cups water. It cooks quickly. Bring to a boil, simmer for about 5 minutes, then turn off heat and let sit for 10 minutes for water to absorb. Place in large bowl, cover, and refrigerate at least 2 hours.

A couple of hours later, prepare the vegetables for the salad. Color is the key to beautiful quinoa salad. You'll want about 4-6 cups total of colorful vegetables. To reflect the delicacy of the grain, they should all be fairly delicate, chopped small or sliced thin. The greens, peppers, carrot, cabbage, onion, and cucumbers are the most important ingredients. You can choose any of these:

chopped raw beets

thinly sliced radishes

quartered and sliced cucumbers with the skins left on

thinly sliced and slightly chopped red cabbage

thinly sliced red onions

green, red, and yellow sweet peppers chopped small

at least 1 cup finely chopped raw or lightly steamed greens

fresh pea pods or sugar peas, raw or lightly steamed

fresh raw or lightly steamed asparagus

artichoke hearts chopped small

scallions sliced thin

Jerusalem artichokes thinly sliced

grilled portabella mushroom, chopped

grated carrot

The dressing is 1/4 cup olive oil and 1/8 cup ume plum vinegar. Pour over salad and toss. If you can't find ume plum vinegar at a health food store or Asian specialty store, you could use one of the lighter balsamic vinegars, the amount may be reduced.

Garnish with fresh cilantro leaves (optional) and serve within a few hours.

While teaching classes, entertaining friends, or hoping to inspe clients, I often need to prepare food for people who are new to whole grains and natural food. This salad is one of my favorites for those occasions. Quinoa is an unusual grain that not many have encountered. It has a light, sweet, mild taste that is appealing to people who may not like he more dense whole grains. Using really colorful fresh vegetables makes the salad very appealing and seem like something festive, rather than just health food.

Ume plum vinegar seems to have solid appeal to those who are not used to vinegars, and who are accustomed to more conventional fare. So it makes a good dressing for this salad, something very different, but in an intriguing positive way.

The end result is a positive experience - leading to more interest in whole foods and healthy choices.

Quinoa is a quick cooking grain, helpful when you don't have time to prepare rice. It even serves well as a breakfast food, cooked as usual and maple syrup, yogurt, nuts and fruit are all great additions.

Traditional Spinach Salad

Serves: 2-4
Time: 15 minutes
Type of dish: side or
  main
Equipment: basic,
  an egg slicer is
  convenient
Leftovers: will not
  keep well
Ingredients: 1
  bunch fresh
  spinach, eggs,
  Mandarin
  oranges,
  cashews, olive
  oil, honey, red
  wine vinegar

Sort through, wash, and dry with a towel one bunch fresh (not frozen) spinach. Tear into bite sized pieces, or leave whole if the leaves are not too large. Place the spinach in a salad bowel.

Arrange the following ingredients on the greens in a nice pattern. 1/2 pound crumbled feta cheese (use your hands to break up the chunks), 3 sliced hard boiled eggs, a few shakes non-meat fake bacon (optional), Mandarin orange slices from two oranges, and sliced cashews. You can also add small bread croutons if desired.

In a jar with a lid, combine 1/3 cup olive oil with 1 T honey, 2 pinches of salt (about 1/8 t), 3 T red wine vinegar. Shake and pour over the salad serve right away once the dressing has been applied.

To make this nontraditional use wild greens (dandelion, lamb's quarters) instead or combine spinach with other wild salad greens.

How to hard boil an egg: Place eggs in a small sauce pan, cover with cold water. Bring to a boil. Let simmer for 10 minutes, uncovered. Turn off heat. Let sit for 10 minutes. Rinse with cold water. Hard boiled eggs can be refrigerated for about a week.

Steamed Salad

Serves: 4
Time: 20 minutes
Type of dish: side
Equipment: steamer, grater
Leftovers: do not freeze, not
    good as a leftover.
Ingredients: red cabbage,
    two kinds of kale, two
    kinds of chard, carrot,
    radish, red onion, clove
    oil, light vinegar

In batches, steam about 1-2 minutes each, until the color changes but not hardly wilted: 2 cups red cabbage, chopped into fairly large but still bite sized pieces, about four large leaves Russian kale, about four large leaves other kale, about four large leaves green Swiss chard, about four large leaves red leafed chard each torn into smaller pieces.

Plunge into cold water as you remove the greens from the steamer. Let drip dry in a colander, then pat dry with a towel.

Place greens in a salad bowl. Add one cup grated carrots, 2 slivered red radishes (can be omitted), 1/2 red onion, slivered.

Dress with 2 T olive oil and 1 T light vinegar, red wine is great. If you want to be fancier, use walnut oil in place of olive oil, and 1 T of lemon juice.

The greens could also be very briefly sauted in a bit of oil instead of steaming, add no oil at the end, just a dash of lemon juice.

Pesto

Serves: 4-6
Time: about 10 minutes to
    prepare
Type of dish: side or main
Equipment: food processor
Leftovers: freezes well, use
    refrigerated pesto
    within 2-3 days
Ingredients: 1 quart very
    fresh greens, garlic,
    olive oil, nuts, cheese
    (optional)

In a food processor fill the container with freshly picked greens that have been rinsed, inspected and dried off, about 1 quart or more. Yellow dock, dandelion and lambs quarters, are some unusual greens that make great pesto. Add 3-4 whole garlic cloves. Drizzle about 1/4 cup of olive oil over the leaves.

Add 1/2 cup of the nuts of your choice; walnuts, pecans, and pine nuts are all favorites. Run the food processor at medium speed. Use a spatula to frequently scrape down the sides. If it isn't easily forming a paste within a minute or so, add more oil. Use immediately on hot pasta, in a cold pasta salad, as a condiment on a sandwich, or any other use. This can also be frozen in plastic bags or small containers. For best results use frozen pesto within 6 months. I add cheese (parmesan or romano) as I use the pesto, rather than freezing it with the cheese mixed in. You may prefer to add the cheese while you're making it.

Pesto made from yellow dock leaves is a spring favorite of mine. The yellow dock leaves come early, way before any basil, and in early may I have enough to freeze many pints of pesto and to enjoy it fresh on hot pasta.

Pesto made from wild plants is has an unexpected fresh taste, and some people come to prefer it to using traditional basil. There are so many plants to experiment with, don't be tied to tradition. I look forward to garlic mustard pesto next spring.

Colorful Coleslaw

Serves: 4-6
Time::15 minutes to prepare, 24
    hours to marinate
Type of dish: side
Equipment: a grater and a large
    wide mouthed jar will be
    helpful
Leftovers: use within 1-3 days
Ingredients: red cabbage, 1/2
    bunch fresh greens, carrots,
    onion, apple cider vinegar,
    sugar, olive oil.

In a large bowl mix together 3 cups thinly sliced and then chopped red cabbage, 2 cups grated carrot, 1/2 white onion thinly sliced and then chopped (about 1/4-1/2 cup), 2 cups chopped raw greens (chard, spinach, kale, lambs quarters, or a combination including some wild greens).

In a small bowl combine 1/2 cup apple cider vinegar, 1/2 cup water, 1/4-1/2 cup sugar (depending on taste), and 2 T olive oil. Stir so the sugar is fully dissolved. Pour over vegetables, and mix well.

The easiest way to age this salad is to put it in a wide mouthed half-gallon or larger jar. Use a plastic lid, or place a plastic bag or wax paper between the jar and the lid. Store on its side in the refrigerator, turning and shaking frequently for 24 hours. A half gallon wide mouthed canning jar works well. You can also use a gallon jar obtained from a restaurant. If a jar is not available store in a tightly covered non metal bowl and stir frequently.

Let this marinate for at least 24 hours before enjoying.

Stir Fries and Skillet Dishes

Stir fries are quick and easy. This is one of the most common way for people to add greens to their meals, and greens are the perfect addition to most stir fries.

Using a well seasoned wok will make stir fries easier, the shape is perfect for tossing ingredients so that they will stay in the pan. With a frying pan or skillet, I tend to underestimate the amount of ingredients I end up using, and things get tossed onto the stove and don't stay in the pan. A wok also concentrates the heat perfectly. Even if you are preparing small dinners, the wok is a great tool for your kitchen.

For the skillet, I rely on my cast iron skillets for nearly all my sauteing and skillet cooking. A well seasoned cast iron pan is easy to clean, distributes heat well, and can even contribute a bit of iron to what you are preparing. Cast iron is also the best for dry roasting. It is hard to do with a regular pan.

No stick surfaces tend to end up scraped and damaged in my kitchen, and aluminum has to be coated to be non-reactive with many foods. Stainless is my second choice if cast iron is not available.

There are a few tricks to a successful stir fry. That information is followed by some more exact recipes.

Stir Fries

Stir fried greens are quick and easy. Adding fat to greens is a common practice throughout the world. Stir fries are a part of many cultures. A variety of ethnic tastes use the stir fry – Chinese being one of the most popular. The following are some ideas and inspiration to create great stir fries, and I've included some specific recipes for beginners.

Use the best quality oil. Olive oil is perfect. Do not reuse the oil, do not use oil that has been previously heated as the chemical changes are not healthy.

Greens reduce in volume when they are cooked. This effect is especially dramatic in stir fries.

The key to a good stir fry is having everything prepared ahead of time, and the order in which you add ingredients. There is a reason that so many stir fries start with onions. Simply cooking onions in a bit of oil brings out the flavor, and creates an aromatic and texturally appealing base for the meal.

Add the ingredients that need the longest cooking time first. Many spices also do well with being the first in the pan, as a minute of cooking in oil brings out their flavor. If you are using onions, garlic, and spices start with them. Food that likes to brown including tempeh, tofu and some winter vegetables can all be added next.

Add vegetables like broccoli, brussel sprouts, cabbage, and other medium soft foods in the middle. The timing will also depend if you want them well cooked or still crunchy. The later you add them, the crunchier they will be.

Near the end of the cooking time add more juicy vegetables like summer squash, also food that doesn't need as long to cook, including the greens.

At the last minute add already cooked food such as cooked pasta, cooked grains, and cooked beans. This is also the time to add herbs, sprouts, miso, and other ingredients that should have just a bit of heat but not actually cook.

Possible stir fry ingredients include: any type of green except lettuces, turnips, beets, summer and winter squash (peel and cube winter squash), pea pods, fresh beans, carrot, all varieties of cabbage, nuts, seeds, broccoli, Jerusalem artichokes (sunchokes), tomatoes, potatoes, sprouts, daikon radish, seaweed, mushrooms, asparagus, eggplant, sweet peppers, chili peppers, eggs, and so much more.

A simple way to get a lot of flavor from a stir fry is to use a prepared oil or paste in the early stages. You can buy pastes just for this purpose. Look in the Thai or Indian foods section of a grocery store fro a variety to choose from. You can also try these two recipes.

The great thing about both of these recipes is that the time consuming task of preparing them is done all at once, and the result can be used for the next month. It then takes almost no time to achieve a rich interesting flavor with just a spoonful of prepared oil.

Chili Garlic Oil

Use a blender, food processor, or blender stick. Blend 1 cup olive oil, 3 T (or more) chili powder, 8 cloves of garlic minced. Be careful not to inhale this as you blend it.

Let mixture sit for 2-3 days before you use it. Use 1-2 T in stir fries in place of other oil. Stores well for a month.

Instead of using chili powder, you can use whole fresh or died chilies. For a milder version use 3-4 banana peppers and 1 cayenne pepper.

> Serves: makes just over a
>   cup of sauce, use 1-2 T
>   per recipe
> Time: 5 minutes to prepare,
>   2-3 days before using
> Type of dish: sauce
> Equipment: blender, food
>   processor or blender
>   stick
> Leftovers: use within a
>   month, keep
>   refrigerated.
> Ingredients: olive oil, chili
>   powder, garlic

Chipolte, Jabanero, and other peppers can be used for hotter versions. Using a variety of what is available makes for a more interesting and intense flavor. I like to use one each of a mild, medium, and hot pepper.

Using dried peppers will help this to keep longer. If you use fresh, use the oil within two weeks.

Ethiopian Berbere Sauce

Serves: makes just over a cup of sauce, use 1-2 T per recipe
Time: 15-20 minutes to prepare, 2-3 days before using
Type of dish: sauce
Equipment: cast iron skillet for dry roasting, spice grinder or mortar and pestle
Leftovers: use within a month, keep refrigerated.
Ingredients: whole seeds of cumin, cardamon, peppercorn, fenugreek; whole cloves, dried chiles, ground nutmeg, tumeric, cinnamon, salt, garlic, ginger, olive oil, red wine

Mix together 2 t whole cumin seed, 5 whole cloves, 1/4 t cardamon seeds, 1/4 t black peppercorns, 1 t whole fenugreek seeds, finely chopped cayenne pepper (optional). Heat a small frying pan and dry roast all the seeds about 1-2 minutes. They should just begin to smell wonderful. Remove from heat as soon as they start to brown or discolor, you do not want them to roast that much.

Let these spices cool while you grind 2-3 dried chiles in a spice grinder. Place in a small glass or plastic container. Add to it 1/2 t ground nutmeg, 1 t ground tumeric, 1/2 t cinnamon, 2 t salt, 2-4 cloves of garlic minced or pressed, 1 t freshly grated ginger, 1/2 cup olive oil, 1/2 cup dry red wine (can be omitted - use more oil in place).

Grind the cooled toasted spices in the spice grinder. Add to the other ingredients. Add powdered cayenne pepper if desired, 1-3 t. Stir well. Let sit 2-3 days before using. Keep refrigerated. Use 1-2 T in stir fries in place of other oil.

Scrambled Eggs and Greens

Serves: 2
Time: 15-20 minutes
Type of dish: main
Equipment: basic
Leftovers: best eaten right away
Ingredients: olive oil, onion,
    green pepper, mushrooms,
    1/2 bunch or 1/2 package
    frozen greens, eggs, milk,
    cheese, tortillas and salsa

In a heavy skillet (such as cast iron) or in your favorite scrambled egg making pan, heat 1-2 T olive oil. Stir in 2 slices onion. Let that cook a few seconds while you chop 1/2 green pepper and add that.

While that cooks wash four moon-light mushrooms and slice them, add that to the pan. While that cooks, wash and tear into small pieces 1/2 bunch of greens or use 1/2 package frozen greens. Chard, collards, kale, spinach, mustard, turnip, beet, and most wild greens work well. Stirring occasionally, break four eggs into a small bowl with a splash of milk. Whip together with a whisk or fork. Add that to the pan, and lower the heat.

While that cooks, and stirring more often, add about 1/4 cup of cubed or grated or crumbled cheese (cheddar, jack, feta, or other). Season with a pinch of salt or a small splash of tamari.

Tastes great with a heated whole wheat tortilla with salsa.

Heat tortillas by placing under the broiler for a about 30 seconds a side, or heat in a dry pan, flipping every 20-30 seconds until warm or use place on a gas burner on direct flame (watch carefully – they need about 5-10 seconds only and catch fire around the edges easily) or toast in a toaster oven. The toaster oven method has caused me to lose a lot of toaster ovens – I seem to have a lot of fires, although most people don't seem to have this problem.

Dandelion Greens

Serves: 4
Time: 30 minutes
Type of dish: side
Equipment: basic
Leftovers: reheats well, best
    used within 2-3 days
Ingredients: 2 bunches
    dandelion or other
    bitter greens, garlic,
    onions or leeks or
    scallions (optional),
    pine nuts or walnuts,
    olives (optional)

Choose large leafed, milder tasting greens.
Use two bunches. Heat about 2 T olive oil
in sauce pan. Add 3-4 garlic cloves, minced
or pressed. If desired you can also add 1-3
leeks, a half bunch of scallions, or 1/2
onion thinly sliced.

Cook on moderate high heat until tender.
Stir in 1/4 cup pine nuts (you can substitute walnuts). Let that cook about 1-2
minutes, then add dandelions that have been rinsed, and ripped or cut
into 1-2 inch pieces. Do not dry. The water on the dandelions helps
them to cook. Turn the heat to low, and cook until wilted, about 5-10
minutes. Stir occasionally. Sprinkle with vinegar (about 1 T).

*Some people enjoy adding olives (1/4 cup pitted and sliced) just after
the pine nuts.*

*If needed, the bitter taste of the dandelions is offset by adding yogurt
after cooking (1/4 cup)*

*Try this with most other greens you have on hand, combine different
greens, or moderate the dandelions with 1/2 and 1/2 dandelion and
spinach, or kale, etc.*

Ginger Greens

Serves: 2-4
Time: 20-30 minutes
Type of dish: side
Equipment: basic
Leftovers: reheats well, best
    used within 2-3 days
Ingredients: olive oil,
    ginger root, 1 bunch
    greens

In a large sauce pan heat 2 T olive oil over medium high heat. Add one thinly sliced onion and then about 2 inches of peeled and thinly sliced and chopped fresh ginger.

Saute lightly and add 1 bunch kale, collards, chard, spinach, or similar greens cut or torn into small bite sized pieces. Do not dry them after rinsing, as the excess water will help them cook.

Cook uncovered over low heat about 10 to 15 minutes until greens are very soft. Add more water if needed, and stir a couple times.

Ginger root can be frozen whole and then used as needed.

Hot Pasta Greens

Serves: 4
Time: 20-30 minutes
Type of dish: side or main
Equipment: basic
Leftovers: reheats well, best
    used within 2-3 days
Ingredients: pasta, 1 bunch
    greens, olive oil
    (optional), feta cheese

Bring 2 quarts of water to boil. Add about four cups (10-12 ounces) of a favorite pasta – shells, linguine, spirals, etc. Use spinach, artichoke flour, or semolina. Cook until al dente – it should not be overcooked and slimy. Follow package directions, and test frequently. Drain.

While that is cooking, saute a bunch of greens (nearly any will serve, also feel free to mix and match. I like to use collards and kale primarily, and add a few wild ones) in about 2 T olive oil. You can also water saute if you'd like to avoid the oil or use unheated oil in final stages. Cook until wilted, reduced in size and a brighter green color.

Combine everything in a serving bowl and add with crumbled feta cheese.

Greens with Garbanzos

Serves: 4
Time: 30-40 minutes
Type of dish: main or side
Equipment: basic
Leftovers: reheats easily, can
    be frozen
Ingredients: 1 bunch greens or
    1 package frozen, olive
    oil, garlic, ginger, cumin,
    coriander, cloves,
    cinnamon, tumeric, chili
    (optional)

Wash and chop one bunch kale, collards, or similar greens, or use a 10 oz. frozen package. In a large skillet heat 2 T olive oil. On medium high heat, add 2 cloves garlic, pressed or diced. Add a one inch piece fresh ginger, peeled and sliced thin and chopped

As that cooks, Add 1 t ground cumin, 1/2 t ground coriander, 1/4 t ground cloves, 1/4 t cinnamon, 1 t tumeric powder, 1 small dried or fresh chili, diced fine or ground (optional)

Saute a minute or two. Add 2 cups cooked garbanzo beans (chickpeas), or one small can. Add greens. Saute until greens are wilted, have changed color, and reduced in size, about 15-30 minutes.

To cook garbanzo beans use the instructions on page 97 for cooking kidney and pinto beans. It is the same.

Risotto Greens

Serves: 4
Time: 20-30 minutes
Type of dish: side or main
Equipment: basic
Leftovers: reheats well, best used
    within 2-3 days
Ingredients: olive oil, onion, garlic,
    risotto, 1 1/2 bunches greens or
    1 1/2 packages frozen, pine nuts
    or walnuts,

In about 2 T olive oil, saute   a medium onion that has been thinly sliced, and then chopped small. Add 2 cloves garlic, pressed or very thinly sliced and minced.

When this is soft and pungent (about 1-3 minutes) add 1 cup risotto, and cook for about a minute to toast the grain. Add water (or vegetable stock) 1/2 cup at a time, until the risotto is plump, al dente, and no more water is absorbed – about 4 cups of liquid, but it will vary by 1-2 cups. Stir in between 1/4 to 1/2 cups nuts, such as walnut or pine nuts.

In a separate pan, steam or boil one to 1 1/2 bunches greens or 1 to 1 1/2 packages frozen greens . Spinach, collards, kale, all are good choices. Chop into small bite sized pieces before cooking. Add cooked greens to risotto mixture. Cook together for about another minute.

Risotto is a rice high in starch. When properly cooked it resembles slightly undercooked pasta.

The first time I encountered risotto was during a business trip that included the treat of a fancy Italian restaurant. Risotto was the side dish to my meal. I had never had risotto before. Thankfully, another guest was familiar with it and when she saw me eating it with a puzzled expression she let me know that this was undercooked, and the worst risotto she had ever encountered. She then engaged in an argument with the waiter, who would not concede that there was something wrong with the dish.
I avoided it until a friend sent me a box of the rice, and I tried cooking it on my own. The result was creamy, texturally pleasing, and tasty. Indeed, my dinner companion had been right. The strange bitter and hard dish we had tried to eat was not properly prepared.
Since then I've enjoyed this quick cooking grain in many forms, from the traditional Italian Arborio rice to the many variations available.

Spanish rice

Start by cooking the rice. In a large sauce pan combine two cups short grain brown rice with four cups water, bring to a boil, simmer still covered for 20 minutes, let sit for 20 minutes.

Meanwhile, heat 4 T olive oil in a wok or very large skillet. Saute 1 large yellow onion, coarsely chopped. If you want this spicy, add finely minced fresh or dried chillies with the onion. Cayenne, jalapeno, almost any chili does well. If you use chilies at this point, omit the chili powder mentioned further on.

Serves: 4-6
Time: 40 minutes,
*   including cooking rice*
Type of dish: side or main
Equipment: basic
Leftovers: reheats well, use
*   within 3-4 days.*
*   Freezes well.*
Ingredients: brown rice,
*   olive oil, onion, chilies*
*   or chili powder*
*   (optional), cinnamon,*
*   cloves, cumin, parsley*
*   or cilantro (optional),*
*   fresh or canned*
*   tomatoes, 1 bunch*
*   greens or 1 package*
*   frozen*

As the onion begins to soften, add 1 sweet pepper, chopped. When the pepper starts to soften, add 1/2 t ground cinnamon, 1/4 t ground cloves, 1/2 –2 t chili powder (depending on your taste – can also be omitted), 1-2 t crushed dried basil, 1 t ground cumin, 1/4 cup chopped fresh parsley and/or 2 T fresh cilantro (can be omitted).

Stir in the seasonings and let them heat. Add 1 bunch of greens – mustards, collards, spinach, kale, collards, or others. They should be finely chopped, most or all of the rib removed. Or use 1 package frozen greens. Add one large (14 oz.) can diced or crushed tomatoes, or 4-6 chopped fresh tomatoes.

Cover and let cook on low heat for 15 minutes. If you use fresh tomatoes, you may need to add a few T of water to prevent sticking. Add rice to the skillet and mix well, if there isn't room then combine in larger sauce pan. Heat on very low heat for another 15 minutes, watching to make sure the bottom doesn't burn. You may need to turn off the heat and just let this sit to blend the flavors.

Aromatic Greens

Serves: 4-6
Time::5 minutes to prepare,
    20-30 to cook
Type of dish: side
Equipment: basic
Leftovers: use within 3
    days, can be frozen.
Ingredients: asafetida,
    cumin, coriander,
    cardamon, cloves,
    cinnamon, tumeric, 2
    bunches greens or 2
    packages frozen.

In a large skillet, use about 1 cup of water. Add 1/8 t asafetida, 2 t ground cumin, 1 t ground coriander, 1 t ground cardamon seeds, 1/2 t ground cloves, 1/2 t ground cinnamon, 1 t tumeric.

While simmering wash and sort through two bunches greens. Spinach, kale or collards are best. Tear or chop into bite sized pieces. Or use 2 packages frozen greens. Add to skillet, and cover. The cover may not fit right away, stir occasionally until they are reduced in size and the cover settles. Let saute covered, on low heat for at least 20 minutes or until very tender. Stir a few times, add more water if needed.

Remove from heat and blend in about 3/4 cup yogurt.

In place of the water, use 2 T olive oil. Heat the spices until they pop, and are very fragrant, about 2 minutes. Add the greens, pour additional water over them (about 3/4 cup), and proceed as above.

It is worth the trouble to buy whole spices, and grind your own. A mortar and pestle is fine, or dedicate a small coffee grinder as a spice grinder. It takes almost no extra time, and the result is fresher spices, better flavor, and often the whole spices are a little less expensive as well. The tumeric and asafetida -- is purchased already ground.

Of all the recipes in this book, this may be my favorite. It is quick, easy, and the greens are infused with the spices as they turn buttery soft. This recipe is inspired by the many Indian style recipes for spinach.
Like the recipe for quinoa salad, I frequently make this dish for students and friends who may never had tried collards and kale before. It is fragrant, has a rich feel, and just tastes wonderful.

Soups

Greens and soups go so easily together. The greens melt into the background, all of the nutrients are in the stock rather than in water that is removed, and the slow cooking brings out the savory quality of most greens.

Dal combines the protein in easily digested lentils with warm and welcoming spices that can be either spicy or complex or both. It is a versatile food, that can be served as a soup, over grains, or scooped with bread.

There are hundreds of good soup recipes, but the most easily made or those with ingredients close at hand. Once you've made soup a couple of times, it becomes easy to improvise.

Vegetarian Soup Stock

In the previous recipes you will have water left over from steaming and boiling greens, bits and pieces of greens or vegetables that may be too tough for your current recipe but that are still perfectly good, and other left over juices and parts.

A good soup stock is a collection of many past parts of meals. Unless you make soup at least once a week you'll need to freeze all these leftovers for when you do want to make a hearty soup. You can keep a large sized plastic container in your freezer that will hold a quart or two of stock ingredients. Just keep adding to it until you have enough or when you make soup again – whichever comes first.

Avoid using a lot of the mid ribs and ends of greens, because the flavor of the stock may be more bitter. The water from steaming or boiling greens is a great addition, vegetables or greens that you can't use before they go bad, all can go into the freezer for a later soup.

Soup stock can also be made from bouillon cubes, low or no salt is available, and their are many vegetarian bouillon cubes that are very flavorful.

Depending on the soup you intend to make, you can use water instead of stock, or even make your own fresh soup stock. A simple soup stock can be made by adding onion, carrot, celery, garlic, and other vegetables to water and simmering fro an hour or two. The garlic and onion can be sauted in advance, or just added to the water to cook.

Dal

Serves: 4
Time: about 45 minutes
Type of dish: side or main
Equipment: basic, strainer
  helps
Leftovers: freezes well,
  stores in the
  refrigerator up to 3-5
  days
Ingredients: lentils, onion,
  1 bunch greens or 1
  package frozen, ginger,
  cinnamon stick,
  cardamon seeds,
  coriander seeds, cumin
  seeds, tumeric,
  asafetida

Carefully rinse and sort through 2 cups lentils – red, yellow, or brown. The yellow split pea is especially pretty with the greens mixed in. Remove any stones, hulls, or other debris. Rinse the lentils by placing them in a strainer and running water over them, or put them in the pan you'll be using, fill it with water, swish it around, and then pour most of the water out. Repeat until the water is pretty clean, and not foamy or scummy. It may take 1-4 times.

Put the cleaned lentils in a pot with 2-3 times the amount of water as lentils. Bring to a simmer. Add a thinly sliced onion (you can saute it in olive oil if you'd like, or add raw), 1-3 cloves pressed garlic, 1/2 can crushed tomato (optional), 1 bunch greens (almost any kind) torn or cut into small pieces. 1 inch fresh ginger, peeled and sliced thinly. Cook the dal and greens on medium to medium low heat until they are very soft, about 20-30 minutes.

Make a fresh ground garam masala from 4 cloves, 1/2 stick cinnamon, 1/2 t cardamon seeds, 1/2 t coriander seeds, 1 1/2 t cumin seeds ground in a spice grinder. Add 1/2 t tumeric powder and a tiny pinch asafetida powder.

Stir the garam masala into the cooked dal. Let it sit a few minutes This can be served as a soup, or poured over brown rice or other grain.

Gazpacho

Serves: 4
Time: 15-20 minutes to
    prepare, 1-3 hours to
    chill.
Type of dish: side or main
Equipment: blender or food
    processor
Leftovers: does not keep
    well, use right away or
    the next day at most.
Ingredients: onion,
    cucumber, garlic,
    green pepper, basil
    oregano, thyme, olive
    oil, wine vinegar,
    lemon juice, cumin,
    fresh tomatoes, 1-2
    cups greens, garnishes

The only time to make gazpacho is in season. Don't try this in the winter!

In a food processor blender lightly pulse 1/2 medium onion thickly sliced, 1 medium cucumber in chunks, 2 cloves garlic, 1 green pepper in chunks. 1/4 t each basil, oregano, and thyme. 1/4 cup olive oil, 1/4 cup wine vinegar, juice from 1 lemon (about 2 T), 1/2 t salt, 1 t ground cumin, three fresh tomatoes (suggested) or 1 can plum tomatoes with juice (if you have no other option). 1-2 cups spinach, swiss chard, kale, non-bitter dandelion, lambs quarters or yellow dock – or a combination of these torn into smaller pieces.

Pulse until the ingredients are well mixed, and reduced in size but not liquefied. Let this chill in the refrigerator for 1-3 hours before serving, to integrate the ingredients.

Traditional garnishes are croutons, sour cream, slice of lemon, slice of avocado, a spear of cucumber.

How to juice a lemon: roll the lemon with some force on a hard surface, for example a cutting board or your counter. The hard outer peel should feel softer. Cut in half at the small diameter. Ideally you would have a lemon juicer – that you then use to ream out the inside and strain the seeds. If not, squeeze it over a small bowl, let the seeds squeeze out as well, and fish them out with a spoon when you're done. It is important to remove the rind, the seeds, and any of the white stuff from your juice as that gives a bitter taste.

Butternut Squash Soup

Serves: 4
Time: an hour to bake
  squash, about 30-40
  minutes to preapre and
  cook soup
Type of dish: side or main
Equipment: blender or food
  processor
Leftovers: refrigerate for 2-
  3 days, not as good
  after freezing
Ingredients: butternut
  squash, 1 bunch greens
  or 1 package frozen,
  milk, nutmeg

Slice a butternut squash lengthwise. Scoop out the seeds and the gooey membrane around the seeds. Place the halves cut side down on a baking sheet. Bake for 1 hour at 350 degrees, until very soft but not falling apart. Remove from oven use a hot pad to flip cut side up, let cool.

While the squash is cooling, prepare 1 bunch of greens by washing, sorting, and tearing or chopping into bite sized pieces. Or use 1 package frozen greens and omit this step. If using hardier greens like kale or collards, lightly steam them. Frozen greens and greens such as spinach or chard can be added directly once the squash is pureed.

When the squash is cool enough to handle, scoop it into a food processor or blender. Slowly add 2 cups of milk. To minimize splashing, pulse to start, and then as it is integrated mix thoroughly for 30 seconds to a minute until smooth.

Pour the blended squash into a medium sized sauce pan. Add the greens, either steamed or raw. Heat on low heat for about 20-30 minutes, until the greens are cooked. Do not let the soup boil. If it seems too thick, add water.

Serve with a sprinkle of fresh nutmeg for each bowl.

1 onion, sauted in olive oil until soft, can be added before you puree the squash.

Rice milk, water, soymilk, and yogurt can all be substituted for the milk used in the recipe.

This is such a beautiful soup, the rich orange color contrasting with the pieces of greens. For the longest t ime I made this without the greens, the day that I was inspired to add some frozen lambs quarters I was just delighted by the effect and have included greens ever since.

Big Pot of No Carne Chili

Serves: 10-12
Time: once the beans are cooked, about
        15 minutes to prepare and another
        30 minutes to cook
Type of dish: main
Equipment: basic
Leftovers: great as leftovers, keeps 3-5
        days, freezes well.
Ingredients: pinto and/or kidney beans,
        canned or fresh tomatoes, wine
        (optional), carrots, onion, green
        pepper (optional), celery, cayenne,
        chili, clove, cinnamon, basil,
        oregano, cilantro, cumin, tamari,
        bulgur

Prepare kidney or pinto beans, I like to combine them half and half. You can use canned beans and skip this step, but that adds dollars to the cost of the whole thing.

To prepare the beans, take 3 cups of dried beans, rinse well by running water over them while in a strainer, or place the beans in the large pot you will use, fill with water, swish them around, and drain. Repeat until water is clear, 1-3 times. Look for and remove rocks, or what are called "dead" beans - anything that is discolored or otherwise not normal. Fill the pot with water at least 4 inches above the beans. You have two options. The quick method is to bring the beans and water to a boil, turn off the heat and let sit for two hours, drain off the water, and proceed to cooking. The longer option is to fill the pot as above, but let it sit overnight, drain off the water, and proceed with cooking. This is to minimize the gassy effect. I find that the longer method works better.

Once the beans have set, drain the water. Refill with fresh water, an inch or two above the level of the beans. If you have it, add a small (1-2 inch) piece of tough seaweed, such as kombu. This also helps the beans to be less gassy. Too much seaweed and the beans are slimy. Cook for 1-2 hours, over medium low heat. You want to keep testing until you have a bean that doesn't fall apart, but is soft enough that you can mash it with your tongue against the roof of your mouth.

Drain out the water. Some people reserve some for the chili, but I think it has an off taste that is starchy and beany that doesn't go well. To the bean mixture add 2 28 oz. cans tomatoes – crushed, whole, puree, or a combination. The puree makes a smoother chili, I prefer the crushed or whole. I mash the whole ones with the spoon while it cooks. Stir in 1/4 cup red wine (optional), 1 cup chopped carrots, 1 large onion, chopped, 1 sweet pepper chopped (optional), 1 stalk celery , 2-4 cups water (it should be pretty watery at this point), 1 cayenne pepper, minced (optional), 1-2 chilies dried or fresh (optional), 1 t – 1 T chili powder (optional if you use above peppers), pinch of ground clove, pinch of ground cinnamon, 1 t basil, crushed, 1 t oregano, crushed, 1 t cilantro, minced, 1 t ground cumin, 2 T tamari.

Simmer for 20 – 30 minutes.

Check that it is not very thick, add more water if needed. It should still be somewhat watery because now you will add 1 1/2 cups bulgur. The bulgur will absorb a lot of the water. Let that simmer on very low heat for another 15 minutes.

Cornbread makes a great accompaniment to chili.

This makes enough for a crowd, or you can freeze it and have quick "meal in a bowl" soup all winter. I freeze it in individual oven proof dishes, so it is a convenient frozen food to bake for 30-40 minutes and enjoy. You can also reheat it in a sauce pan, but baked chili is really better – especially if you grate some cheese over the top when you do bake it.

Cornbread

Serves: 4 -6
Time: 30 minutes to
    prepare and bake
Type of dish: side
Equipment: basic - flour
    meal is ideal
Leftovers: best when fresh,
    leftovers can be toasted
    the next day.
Ingredients: cornmeal,
    whole wheat flour,
    baking powder, baking
    soda, salt, yogurt, egg,
    honey or maple syrup.

This doesn't have greens in it, but it goes with this soup, and is one of my most requested recipes.

Heat oven to 450 degrees. If you have a convection oven use it. Butter a 10 inch cast iron skillet, or an 8 inch square glass baking dish.

Mix one cup fresh, good quality yellow cornmeal in a medium sized bowl with 1 cup whole wheat flour (can also use spelt, buckwheat, or whole wheat pastry flour) and 2 t baking powder, 1/2 t salt, 1/2 t baking soda.

In a separate bowl combine 1 cup yogurt (watery is good, if it is very thick dilute it with water) with 1 egg, 1/4 cup honey or maple syrup. Mix these ingredients well.

After the wet ingredients are blended, quickly add to the dry ingredients, scrape the bowl with a spatula and mix with a few strokes – do not over mix. Transfer to the prepared baking dish quickly, as the baking powder begins to react with the wet ingredients. A few shakes should level the dish, or it will even out in the oven.

Bake for 20 minutes, serve immediately.

You can add 1 cup blueberries, or strawberries (fresh or frozen) to the dry mixture.

Another variation is to add 1/2 cup grated cheddar cheese. You may choose to also add 1 small jalapeno sliced very thin with the cheese – it makes a very spicy cornbread, so some people just use the cheese.

See the note on page 60 about using fresh ground corn meal.

Green Soup

Serves: 4
Time: 15 minutes to
    prepare, about 45
    minutes to cook
Type of dish: main
Equipment: basic, optional
    blender, food processor
    or blender stick
Leftovers: freezes well,
    reheats for the next 3-5
    days
Ingredients: olive oil,
    garlic, onion, 1 bunch
    fresh greens or 1
    package frozen,
    vegetable broth,
    tomatoes, cooked
    beans, herbs

Use a large soup pot. On fairly high heat add 2 T olive oil, and saute 1 onion thinly sliced, 2-6 cloves garlic, pressed or minced.

Once the onion is translucent add 1 bunch kale, collards, swiss chard, or other similar green, ripped or cut to make bite size pieces. Stir until slightly wilted, and a brighter green color.

Add 4 cups broth – this could be vegetable broth, water to which vegetables broth seasoning has been added, or your "freezer broth". You can also use plain water, just increase the seasonings.

Add one can chunked or whole tomatoes, or 4-6 fresh tomatoes. Add 2 cups cooked beans – for this soup my favorites in order are garbanzo, navy, black eyed peas, and lima. These can be canned, frozen, or ones that you have cooked.

Season with basil, rosemary, oregano, thyme, and dried or fresh parsley, about 1 t. each. Simmer on low heat for 45 minutes.

For a thicker soup, scoop out a cup or two of the soup, be sure to include plenty of beans. Process in a food processor until smooth, add back to the soup and heat another 5-10 minutes. You can also use a stick blender to partially blend the soup in the pot.

Especially if your broth is a little on the bland side, serve with a t. of miso for each bowl. You can also add a dollop of sour cream or yogurt on top of each serving. A splash of pepper sauce may also be desired. Soups tend to be over salted, so add salt as needed at the table.

Jerusalem Artichoke Soup

Serves: 4
Time: 45 minutes
    including cooking time
Type of dish: main
Equipment: basic
Leftovers: freezes well, in
    the refrigerator will
    keep 3-5 days
Ingredients: soup stock,
    Jerusalem artichokes,
    onion, lemon juice,
    cumin, tarragon, dill
    weed, celery seed, 1
    bunch fresh greens or 1
    package frozen, yogurt
    or milk or soy milk

In a large sauce pan heat together 4 cups soup stock – from vegetable bouillon cubes, "freezer stock" or water. Add 2 cups sliced Jerusalem artichokes sunchokes), 1 onion chopped, a splash of lemon juice, 1/2 t ground cumin, 1 t tarragon, pinch of dill weed, pinch of ground celery seed, 1 bunch greens chopped small (sweeter greens like spinach, collards, swiss chard would work best)

Heat for about 30 minutes, on a slow simmer, until the onion is soft and the greens are coming apart easily. Transfer in batches to a food processor or blender, blend until smooth. Serve at room temperature after adding 1 cup yogurt or 1 cup milk or 1 cup milk substitute such as soy milk. Rice milk doesn't work as well.

Jerusalem Artichokes are also known as sunchokes. Once established, they take over the garden area where they are planted. The plant itself grows 6-8 feet high, with a small yellow sunflower like flower at the top. I have them growing in a corner of my garden, and I harvest nearly 20 pounds a year of the crisp root. They keep coming back, the trick is more to contain them rather than needing to encourage them.

I share the harvest with friends who help me dig. I refrigerate the rest in plastic bags in the crisper. I don't wash them until I want to use them, and then they need to be scrubbed with a vegetable brush to remove all the dirt.

While most cookbooks suggest using the Jerusalem artichoke within a week of purchase, by not washing it letting it sit in the crisper I've had them last for nearly a year, until the next harvest.

They can be used in place of water chestnuts in stir fries, sliced or grated for salads, and they make an interesting earthy tasting sweet soup. They can be cooked and added to mashed potatoes, They are very high in iron, protein, and potassium.

Mushroom Potato Leek Soup

Serves: 6-8
Time:: 15 minutes to
    prepare, 1 hour to
    cook.
Type of dish: main
Equipment: basic
Leftovers: use within 3-5
    days, freezes well
Ingredients: olive oil, leeks,
    mushrooms, potatoes,
    celery)optional),
    cabbage (optional), 1
    bunch fresh greens or 1
    package frozen,
    additional vegetables
    (optional), tamari

In a large soup pot heat 4 T olive oil. Saute 4-6 leeks, thinly sliced, rinsed of all dirt, and using at least half of the green part. Add 1 pound moonlight mushrooms, rinsed, the end of the stem removed, and quartered. Let cook until leeks are very soft.

Add 2 quarts water, or vegetable broth. Scrub 4-5 medium sized potatoes. Leave the skin on, and chop into bite sized pieces. Add to the soup pot.

Add 1 cup chopped celery (optional), 1/2 cup chopped cabbage green or red (optional), 1 bunch greens (mustard, kale, collards, spinach, dandelion, nettles, or swiss chard or a combination) rinsed and chopped into small pieces. You can leave some of the mid rib, as it will be pretty soft.

Use up to 2 cups additional veggies (optional). Whatever vegetables you have laying around – broccoli, green beans, corn, zucchini, yellow squash, carrot, turnips. If you use winter vegetables be sure to cut into pieces smaller than the potatoes. Use up to 2 cups additional veggies.

Season with 1 T Tamari . Cook uncovered for 1 hour. Stir occasionally.

If you like a thicker soup, remove 2-4 cups of the soup after it has cooked for at least 45 minutes, blend into a puree, add back to the soup.

Leeks will have dirt within their inner unexposed layers. You can rinse them after every few slices, or slit the white part lengthwise all the way through before slicing, and thoroughly rinse them as you separate the layers so the water can get between them.

Chilled Greens and Cucumber Soup

Serves: 4-6
Time: about 45 minutes
Type of dish: side or main
Equipment: basic
Leftovers: does not freeze,
   use within 1-2 days
Ingredients: butter or olive
   oil, cumin seed, dill
   seed, green or white
   onions, 3 cups greens
   or 1 1/2 packages
   frozen, cucumber,
   yogurt

Heat 1 T butter or olive oil in a medium sized pot over medium heat. Add 2 t whole cumin seed and 1 t whole dill seed. Stir until the seeds are fragrant and slightly browned, about 1 minute or less. Add about 1 cup thinly sliced green onions, including tops, or one yellow onion sliced very thin. Saute until soft, about 1-3 minutes.

Add 2 cups water, bring to a simmer, Stir in three cups of washed greens – spinach, nettles, dandelion, sorrel, mache, chard, are all good choices or use 1 1/2 packages frozen greens. Let that cook for at least 20 minutes, covered, on medium heat.

Meanwhile, chop 1 medium sized cucumber into chunks Leave peel unless it tastes bitter, remove seeds if they are large. Once the greens are well cooked, add the cucumber. Simmer for another 5 minutes.

Remove from heat. Cool slightly. Puree in a food processor or blender until smooth.

Refrigerate for 2- 3 hours. Stir in one cup yogurt Serve chilled, with additional yogurt on the side.

For a richer soup, use cream or sour cream in place of the yogurt.

Cold soup tends to strike people as either a special unusual treat, or something that just isn't right. If we could call it something other than soup, it might have more success. Chilled Greens and Cucumber Yogurt Blend? It might be better.

Sweet Carrot Soup

Serves: 4 -6
Time: 30 minutes to
    prepare and bake
Type of dish: side
Equipment: basic - flour
    meal is ideal
Leftovers: best when fresh,
    leftovers can be toasted
    the next day.
Ingredients: carrots, butter,
    milk or substitute,
    onion, 2 cups greens,
    nutmeg, allspice

Wash 4 large carrots. Be sure that they are sweet and not old. Slice of the root end. Slice the whole carrot lengthwise, and then slice into thick half round slices. Heat 4 T butter in a large skillet. Add the carrots, and cook until tender over medium to medium low heat, about 15-20 minutes. Stir occasionally.

Remove the carrots from the pan, and allow to cool slightly. When they are cool enough, add to a blender or food processor. Add 1-2 T more butter to the skillet and a thinly sliced small yellow onion. Saute onion on medium heat until slightly browned, about 1-3 minutes. Let that cool slightly, and add to carrots.

Slowly add 2 cups of milk, water, soymilk, or rice milk to the blender or food processor while mixing. Process for a minute or two, until the carrots are finely chopped and the whole thing has a grainy texture.

Steam 2 cups of chopped greens. Choose greens that are sweet or mild in taste – spinach, chard, chickweed, mache, and kale or collards that have gone through a frost are good choices. Steam until well cooked, about 10-20 minutes depending on the greens.

Combine the greens and the carrot mixture in a sauce pan, and heat together on medium low heat without boiling for about 15 minutes. Add 1/4 t ground nutmeg and 1/4 t ground allspice before serving.

Bakes and Casseroles

One of the quickest and easiest ways to prepare greens is to place them in a casserole, or a baked dish. The basic bake takes only minutes to prepare, and then a long hour to cook. Other recipes in this section are elaborate creations that can take up to an hour just to prepare.

Winter is the best season for most of these recipes. The smell of baking vegetables fills the house, an anticipatory and welcome scent.

Bakes

This style of preparing a main dish is especially appealing in the winter. Hearty "winter" vegetables such as potatoes, cabbage, carrots, and winter squash are made savory, soft and satisfying by this method. Greens are an easy and nutrient enriching ingredient.

This is a very quick to prepare dish, (5-10 minutes) but it will take an hour to bake. I use a glass casserole dish with a lid, or a souffle dish covered with aluminum foil.

Possible ingredients include potato chunks, carrot pieces, summer squash, onions, garlic, cabbage, tofu, tempeh, seitan, beets, turnips, rutabaga, parsnips, winter squash (peeled), tomatoes, hot peppers, sweet peppers, broccoli, cauliflower, asparagus, peas, corn, pea pods, pre cooked beans, precooked rice. Any green will do well, especially mustards, kale, and collards. Rip into small pieces.

The veggies on the bottom will get the most juice. I usually place potatoes and onions on the bottom layer. The greens need to be in the middle, so that they stay moist. While this is usually cooked with a lid, sometimes I layer tempeh or tofu on the top and drizzle some olive oil as the last step so that there is a bit of crispness to those ingredients.

When you use greens in this dish, remember that they will reduce in volume. So often the lid won't immediately fit – I just place it on and as the greens cook the lid settles.

The trick to making the bake work well is the flavorings you add. My most common choice is a good vinegar . For more on vinegars see page 141. Mushroom infused vinegars are a favorite for bakes. For a 10 inch round casserole, I use about 1/4 cup. Sometimes I also use a flavored oil. Or sprinkle a bit of olive oil on the top. I may also add a few shakes of Thai chili sauce. For a wetter "stew" texture, add equal parts water and vinegar, with a generous dash of tamari. For a rich taste, I may use 1 cup of yogurt, or 1 cup of sour cream, or a combination of these two. If I add yogurt or sour ream I omit the olive oil, and cut back on the vinegar.

You may also try 1/2 cup yogurt mixed with pre-made or home-made spice mix (pages 83 and 84), 1/2 cup yogurt plain, 1/2 cup milk mixed with an egg, or plain water with garam masala (recipe on page 94).

Simple Winter Bake

Serves: 4-6
Time: 10 minutes to
    prepare, 1 hour to bake
Type of dish: main
Equipment: covered
    casserole
Leftovers: keeps 3-5 days,
    easily reheated, can be
    frozen but textures
    could change so not
    recommended
Ingredients: potatoes,
    onion, greens, broccoli,
    cabbage, tempeh,
    vinegar, olive oil

Use a covered casserole dish, about 10 inch square or slightly larger. If you lack a cover, you can use aluminum foil. Spray with olive oil nonstick spray, or coat with olive oil. Preheat the oven to 375 degrees.

Clean 4 medium potatoes. Cut into chunks and place in casserole. Remove the outer peel from a large onion, slice into thick slices and break up the pieces as you place over the potatoes.

Rinse and rip up into bite sized pieces one bunch of kale or collards. Feel free to use most of the mid ribs, as it will get very tender. Or use one package frozen greens, slightly thawed.

Rinse broccoli, remove the tough first inch of stem. Cut the stem into about one inch chunks. Cut the flowering part into bite sized pieces or slightly larger. Put on top of the greens.

Take a red cabbage and slice about 1/2 inch slices from it, depending on the size, you might want to then slice those long pieces in half. Create about 1 1/2 to 2 cups of chopped cabbage, add to casserole.

Thinly slice 1 package of tempeh, into strips less than 1/4 inch thick. You'll get about 10 strips from most packages. Layer these strips on your vegetable pile to cover the top. Drizzle 1/4 cup of flavored vinegar over the tempeh. Sprinkle about 1 T tamari sauce next. End with 2-3 T of olive oil.

(continued next page)

Cover, bake for 1 hour. Be sure and serve with some of the juice from the bottom, and that each serving has all the layers of vegetables.

How you cut the vegetables can affect their flavor. The following method improves the taste and texture of carrots, summer squash, and other round vegetables. Instead of uniformly cooked circles, these odd shapes seem to hold in more flavor, keeps the squash from falling apart and feeling mushy, and makes carrots more interesting.

For any rounded vegetable with an edible skin, clean with vegetable rush. Do not peel. Cut off both ends near the tips. Place the vegetable horizontally in front of you on the cutting board. Cut the first piece about an inch from the cut end, with the knife at a 45 degree angle. Rotate the vegetable 1/4 turn away from you. Using the same knife angle as your first cut, cut again. Continue rotating, cutting, until you reach the end. The result is a bunch of chunks of vegetables — with a thin side and a wide end.

Quiche with Grain in Place of Crust

Serves: 6
Time: 15 minutes to
    prepare, 30 minutes to
    bake
Type of dish: main
Equipment: casserole dish
Leftovers: does not freeze
    well. Will keep
    refrigerated 3-5 days,
    reheat in oven or eat
    cold.
Ingredients: 1-2 bunches
    fresh greens or 1-2
    packages frozen, eggs,
    cottage cheese fresh
    cheese or ricotta,
    cheddar or Swiss
    cheese, cooked grain,
    salt, bread crumbs
    (optional) paprika

Saute one large chopped onion in 1/2 - 1 cup water or vegetable broth (depending on how many greens you use). Add one to two bunches almost any green – even the bitter greens will be tempered by the cheese and grain. Or use 1-2 packages frozen greens. Cook while stirring over medium heat, until greens are reduced in size, about 10 minutes. Drain well, saving the cooking water for later soups.

While that is cooking, make the custard. In a large mixing bowl, beat 3 eggs. Add 1 cup cottage cheese fresh cheese or ricotta, 1/2 cup cheese (sharp cheddar is best, you can also use swiss, for an interesting taste). Add 3 cups cooked grain (brown rice, millet, quinoa, barley, buckwheat groats, or wheat berries). Mix well, then add greens and 1/2 t salt.

Stir all these ingredients together so that they are well mixed. Oil a 1 1/2 – 2 quart casserole dish. Place the mixture from the bowl into the casserole. Sprinkle with whole wheat bread crumbs (optional) and a sprinkle of paprika

Bake at 350 degrees for 30 minutes, until it has set, and is lightly browned on top.

To be a true quiche, there must be a pastry shell. We've come to associate a rich custard covering vegetables with quiche. The absence of the crust will not prevent most people from considering this a quiche.
Unless you use prepared crusts, the crust represents additional time and a bit of mess. The focus here is on the greens and custard, a crust is not needed to enjoy this quick and easy recipe.

Layered Polenta

Bring about 5 cups of water to a boil in a medium sized sauce pan. While that is heating scrub two medium sized potatoes. Yellow finn, red, or yukon gold work best.

Do not remove the skins. Cut each potato into about 8 medium sized pieces, and add to heating water.

While the potatoes are cooking, wash, sort and then chop two bunches of washed greens – chard, spinach, rapini; or a combination of these with dandelion, mustard, amaranth, or others will work fine. Or use two packages frozen greens. Put all but about 2 cups (not packed) of the greens in with the potatoes. Cook about 15-20 minutes until the potatoes are very tender, and the greens are also well cooked.

Serves: 8
Time: 30 minutes to make polenta, 1 hour to cool, another 10 minutes in preparation and assembly, and 45 minutes to cook.
Type of dish: main
Equipment: having the right sized dishes to cool the polenta and assemble it may be a problem. Three soufle dishes work well. If not available, one 9" x 14" baking dish will work.
Leftovers: great as a left over, reheat in oven, use within 3 days. Do not freeze.
Ingredients: potatoes, 2 bunches fresh greens or 2 packages frozen, cornmeal, mushrooms, olive oil, tomato sauce, cheese

On medium to medium high heat, very slowly add a cup of corn meal to the cooking greens and potatoes, stirring the whole time. Keep stirring for about 15 minutes. The potatoes will start to fall apart, the cornmeal will start to pull together, and eventually it will become a thickened mass, pulling away from the sides and bottom of the pan while you stir. Add salt and pepper to taste (optional).

Divide the polenta mixture between three oiled dishes that are the same size. I use souffle dishes, with one being the final dish that assembled creation will be coked in. Each should hold 1-2 inches of the polenta, and the final dish should be at least 4-5 inches tall. Once it is divided, set aside to cool, about an hour. If you don't have three dishes, pour the whole thing into one baking dish, 9" x 14".

While this cools, prepare a simple tomato sauce, or use a jarred sauce. To make from scratch, see the end of this recipe.

In a large skillet, heat 3 T olive oil. Slice about 1/2 pound fresh mushrooms (moonlight, shitake, portabella, or other) and saute them in the oil over medium heat. Cook about 3-5 minutes, until cooked through. Set aside.

Grate 8 oz. of cheese. A flavorful, somewhat strong tasting cheese that also melts well is best including cheddar, asiago, jack cheese, or other.

With the cooled polenta, cooked mushrooms, torn greens set aside from before, tomato sauce and grated cheese all at the ready, you're ready to assemble this creation.

If you have the three layers, start with one of the layers of polenta as the base and do not remove it from the dish it cooled in. Pour 1/3 of the tomato sauce evenly over the polenta layer. Place the uncooked torn greens evenly over the sauce, and then sprinkle with 1/2 of the grated cheese.

The next layer should slide easily from the dish once inverted, tap it gently a few times if needed. Place the other polenta layer over this, another 1/3 of the tomato sauce, spread the cooked mushrooms, and the final layer of polenta. Spread the remaining sauce over that, and top with the grated cheese.

If you have the one baking dish only then spread the additional greens first, followed by the mushrooms, the tomato sauce and then the cheese.

Bake in a 350 degree oven for 35-40 minutes until the cheese is nicely browned and the tomato sauce is bubbly.

Let cool slightly before serving, lifting all layers with a spatula or large spoon.

Instead of using more of the same greens for between the layers, you can use two cups of wild greens like dandelion, amaranth, lambs quarters, nettles, or other.

Simple Tomato Sauce

Serves: makes about a quart
Time: 1 hour including cooking time
Type of dish: sauce
Equipment: basic
Leftovers: freezes well, use within 3-5 days if refrigerated.
Ingredients: olive oil, onion, garlic, 1 can tomatoes and 1 can tomato sauce, red wine (optional), oregano, basil, cloves, cinnamon, honey, tamari

In a medium sized sauce pan, saute 3 cloves minced garlic in 2 T olive oil. Add 1 small thinly sliced onion. When garlic is starting to brown and onion is soft, add 1 can tomatoes, crushed or whole. If you use whole tomatoes, break them up as it cooks. Add 1 28 oz. can plain tomato sauce. As it heats, add 1/4 cup red wine (optional), T fresh oregano (or 1 T dried), 2 T basil (or 1 T dried), 1/4 t ground cloves and 1/4 t ground cinnamon.

Cook all of this on medium to low heat uncovered for about 30-45 minutes, simmering lightly, until slightly thickened and reduced in volume. Add 1/2 –1 t honey at the end of the cooking time, and salt or tamari to taste.

Favorite Spaghetti Sauce

Most jarred spaghetti sauces are for convenience first, taste second. It is possible to make your own sauce that is convenient, made to your taste preferences, includes great healthy ingredients, and that costs far less than the gourmet sauces people pay 3, 4 and even 5 dollars a quart.

When you have about 15 minutes to prepare, and about 1 1/2 hours to stir occasionally, try adapting this recipe for your taste preferences:

In a large soup pot heat 1/2 cup olive oil. Saute one large onion, sliced and chopped. Midway through, add 2-6 cloves of garlic, chopped into smallish pieces. When it softens, but hasn't yet browned add 1 or 2 carrots, chopped into small pieces.

Serves: 4-6 quarts, depending on amount of vegetables used
Time: 15 minutes to prepare, 1 to 1 1/2 hours to cook
Type of dish: sauce
Equipment: basic
Leftovers: freezing is recommended, use within 3-5 days if refrigerated.
Ingredients: olive oil, onion, garlic, carrot, mushrooms, tempeh, cooked beans (optional), assorted vegetables (optional), 4 28 oz. cans tomatoes (mix whole, crushed and puree), 1-2 bunches greens, oregano, basil, cloves, cinnamon, tarragon, thyme, red wine or red wine vinegar, honey, tamari

You may also want to add 1-2 cups sliced mushrooms, and a package of crumbled, thinly sliced, chopped tempeh.

Other protein options include already cooked (or canned) garbanzo beans or black eyed peas. Other beans are OK but these two seem to go especially well with tomatoes. People eating your sauce may find these surprising, and perhaps unsettling additions.

Include other vegetables you have on hand. Cabbage, brussel sprouts, broccoli, Jerusalem artichokes, peas, fresh beans, corn, are all god choices.

Add 4 28 oz. cans of tomatoes – a combination of puree, crushed, whole, etc. to create the texture you want. Whole tomatoes will make chunkier sauce. All puree will make a smoother tomato base but it is pretty dense. I personally like the combinations.

Rinse the cans with about 1/3 can water each to clean the inside, and add that water to the mixture.

Wash, sort through and tear or chop into bite sized pieces about 2-4 cups frozen or 1-2 bunches fresh greens (collards, kale, spinach, Swiss chard). Add to pot, with 1/4 cup dry red wine or 1/4 cup red wine vinegar.

Add herbs. Fresh basil, oregano tarragon, and thyme are traditional. I like a pinch of ground clove and cinnamon, but not when there is a lot of garlic.

A bit of honey takes the edge off the tart tomatoes. I may add a dash of tamari, but go light on any salt and pepper. It can be added to taste at the table, and if you put a lot of cheese on your finished spaghetti that may be enough salt.

Let simmer for 1 1/2 – 2 hours on very low heat.

Store what you will use in the next few days in the refrigerator. Put the rest into labeled freezer containers and freeze. Makes 4-6 quarts, depending on the amount of vegetables used.

Want to slice a lot of mushrooms quickly? Use an egg slicer. Place the mushroom sideways in the depression meant for eggs (the stem is the tough part, so let that cut last). Firmly bring the wire assembly down on the mushroom. Nice even slices, quickly done.

Lasagna Roll Ups

Serves: 6-8
Time:: 30 minutes to
asemble, 30-40
minutes to cook
Type of dish: main
Equipment: basic, and
toothpicks
Leftovers: reheats well,
refrigerate fro up to 3
days, freezes well.
Ingredients: lasagna
noodles, 1 bunch fresh
greens or 1 package
frozen, eggs,
mozzarella cheese,
ricotta cheese or
cottage cheese or fresh
garlic cheese (recipe
follows), garlic,
prepared tomato sauce
(see previous pages) or
jarred sauce or 1 28 oz.
can of tomatoes

Bring about 1 1/2 gallons of water to boil in a large soup pot. Slowly add about 20 pieces of lasagna noodles. Cook until the noodles are just tender enough that they can be shaped – do not cook until they are done, and do not cook as long as the package instructs. The time will vary, but with most whole wheat, spinach and other whole grain noodles, it will be about 6-8 minutes.

While the water for the noodles is heating , you can start making the filling. In a medium sized frying pan, saute one bunch of greens or 1 package frozen greens. The greens should be chopped into bite sized or smaller pieces. Use just less than 1/2 cup of water to saute the greens enough so they are wilted, limp, and reduced in size, and the water is absorbed..

Let the greens cool slightly while you lightly beat 3 whole eggs in a medium sized bowl Add greens to the eggs. Grate 1/2 pound of mozzarella cheese. Divide in half, and add half the cheese to the green/egg mixture. The rest will be used for topping. Add one pint ricotta cheese or cottage cheese or 1 1/2 cups fresh home-made cheese (see recipe next page).

Mince or press 2-4 gloves of garlic and add to mixture (optional, and leave out if you make the garlic cheese). Mix this all together, I find my hands to be the best tool. This is the filling.

Oil a casserole dish, about 9 inches square, with olive oil or a no stick spray. Preheat your oven to 350 degrees. When the lasagna noodles are ready, strain them into a colander, and rinse with cold water. Be careful not to rip or break the noodles. Lay a noodle flat on a work surface. Spread about 3 T of the filling mixture the length of the noodle. Roll the noodle up, keeping the filling inside. This tends to be a somewhat messy process, just use your hands to hold things together and put a toothpick through the rolled up noodle to help hold it, and transfer it to the casserole dish.

If you lay the noodle flat, (an easier process) you'll have more uniform textures. Stand it upright (so you can see the spiral of the roll as you look into the pan) you'll have more interesting texture and the rolls will be more distinctly separated. Standing up is best.

Roll up about 16 noodles with the filling, the extra lasagna pieces are to ensure you have enough good noodles to choose from. With the pan filled with standing rolled noodles, cover the whole thing by pouring 1 28 oz. can chunky tomato sauce evenly over the top. You can also use a prepared spaghetti sauce, or use the recipe from the previous page. Use a fairly plain sauce, as this has a pretty rich taste.

Finish by spreading the remaining cheese evenly over the top. Place in the oven, uncovered, and bake for about 45 minutes, until the cheese is golden brown. Let stand about 5 minutes before carefully serving with a spatula.

This freezes really well, and some people think is even better the second day.

Vegan alternative – Replace the mozzarella with you favorite soy cheese. Replace the eggs with 3 T tahini. In place of the ricotta cheese, crumble soft tofu, or make your own soy ricotta substitute, by following the cheese directions given next, but use plain soymilk instead of milk. Use only fresh, plain (perishable) soy milk – not the kind processed in boxes.

Fresh Garlic Cheese:

Serves: makes about 2 cups
Time: 15 minutes to make,
    3 hours to drip
Type of dish: side
Equipment: colander,
    cheesecloth, candy
    thermometer
Leftovers: will keep in the
    refrigerator about one
    week.
Ingredients: milk, lemon
    juice, garlic, salt

In a large soup pot bring 1 gallon of cows or goats milk to 180 degrees F. Very slowly stir in 1/2 cup lemon juice, stirring in only one direction. Let sit covered for 10 minutes. While waiting, press or finely slice fresh garlic – about 3-5 cloves depending on taste.

Mix garlic and three pinches of really good quality real salt in a small bowl Line a colander with three layers cheesecloth. Slowly pour the curdled milk in the colander, with a pan under it to catch the whey. Wring the cheesecloth just enough that the curds are covered. Pick up and rinse under running water for a minute or so, to remove some of the lemon. Dump the rinsed curds in with the garlic and salt, knead gently to mix, Knead more for a smoother texture.

Put the curds back into the cheesecloth, tie the cheesecloth closed and place in colander. Weight or hang the cheese. I put a small plate over the curds and weight it with two cast iron frying pans. You can also hang it. After 3 hours or so, remove the cheesecloth and place in a glass jar to store.

Makes about 2 cups, depending on the type of milk used.

Small amounts of the whey are used to ferment foods and it can be used to flavor soups.

What you don't use to cook with can be eaten on crackers, or in sandwiches. Yum! A spreadable garlicy treat!

Fresh Homemade cheese is a quick, simple, and tasty treat. This is one of the most basic cheeses, with lemon juice used as the curding agent. It is normally a bland cheese. The flavor is improved by adding herbs, or in this case garlic. It can be used in most recipes in place of riccotta.
The quality of the milk matters a lot, and being able to use local dairy milk from either a goat or a cow within hours of milking is a revelation in taste and freshness.

Potato Crust Greens

Serves: 4-6
Time: 20-30 minutes to
    prepare, 35-45 minutes
    to bake
Type of dish: main
Equipment: pie pan, grater
Leftovers: great as leftover,
    use within 3 days.
    Does not freeze well.
Ingredients: potatoes,
    onion, olive oil,
    mushrooms, nuts, 2
    bunches fresh greens or
    2 packages frozen,
    cheddar cheese, eggs,
    milk

Grate 2 large potatoes. Salt lightly and let sit in a colander for 10 minutes. Squeeze out excess moisture. Mix potato with 1 egg. Press into well oiled pie pan. Brush lightly with olive oil. Bake for 10 minutes 350 degrees, until lightly browned.

Prepare the center by sauteing one thinly sliced onion in 2 T olive oil until soft. Add 2 cups sliced mushrooms and cook for another 2-3 minutes. Add a handful of pine nuts or chopped walnuts, 2 bunches kale, collards, Swiss chard or spinach (or combination).

Saute everything, until greens are well wilted. Grate 1 to 1 1/2 cups sharp cheddar cheese. Spread 1/4 cup onto the "crust". Pour in the saute. Cover with remaining cheese. Make a custard of 2 eggs, and about 1/2 cup milk, pour over.

Bake for 35-45 minutes in a 350 degree oven, or until set and lightly browned.

This is a very green pie. Other vegetables can be added, such as cauliflower, cabbage, broccoli, brussel sprouts, asparagus, etc.

You may want more protein in this dish. Saute 8 oz. cubed tempeh before the mushrooms, or add 1 cup cooked lima beans or garbanzos to the saute once the greens are wilted.

The idea for a potato crust is from Mollie Katzen's Moosewood Cookbook. She has a recipe for a cauliflower pie with potato crust that is a favorite of mine, and many guests over the years. I offer this simple alternative in tribute to her and her excellent recipes in all of her many cookbooks.

Seitan Loaf

Preheat oven to 350 degrees Prepare a loaf pan by greasing with olive oil. A loaf pan is about 8 x 3 x 5, the same as you use for baking bread. If you don't have one, you can use a baking dish but the flatter loaf will bake more quickly, and may also need additional liquid.

In a large bowl combine 1 cup seitan, crumbled or torn into small pieces, 1 small onion diced, 2 celery stalks diced, 1 bunch any greens, steamed until wilted and reduced in size, 1 egg, 1 cup fine whole wheat bread crumbs, 1/2 cup chopped nuts (walnuts are perfect, almonds are also good, or sunflower seeds), 1/2 ground sage, 1/2 t thyme, 1/2 cup grated carrot, 2 cloves garlic pressed or chopped, 1/4 cup Jerusalem artichokes diced (optional), 1/4 cup grated cabbage (optional), 1/4 cup broccoli stems, diced fine, (optional), dash of tamari.

Serves: 4
Time: 15 minutes to assemble, 45 minutes to bake
Type of dish: main
Equipment: loaf pan, grater
Leftovers: great as leftovers, use within 3 days
Ingredients: seitan, onion, celery, 1 bunch greens or 1 package frozen, 1 egg, whole wheat bread crumbs, nuts, sage, thyme, carrot, garlic, Jerusalem artichokes (optional), cabbage (optional), broccoli (optional), tamari

Mix well, use your hands. If you need more liquid add milk or water. It should be squishy, a little wet but not dripping, but also hold its shape. Press into the loaf pan.

Bake for 45 minutes, more or less depending on liquid. The top should be firm and the edges only lightly browned.

Seitan is a product made from wheat gluten. A simple water and flour dough is alternately washed in hot and then cold water for many minutes, causing the gluten to form and the starch to wash away. The resulting "wheat meat" is usually cooked in a broth for a few hours. It has an interesting full flavor, and pleasant texture. Making it at home is inexpensive and labor intensive, it can also be purchased at most natural food stores. It can be kept frozen until ready to use.

Twice Baked Potatoes

Serves: 4
Time: 1 1/4 hours total
     baking time, 15
     minutes to prepare
Type of dish: main
Equipment: basic
Leftovers: great as
     leftovers, use within 3
     days, can be frozen
     before final baking
Ingredients: baking
     potatoes, onion, sweet
     pepper, carrot, cabbage,
     1/2 bunch greens fresh
     or 1/2 package frozen,
     garlic, small cooked
     beans (optional), nuts,
     yogurt or milk or
     soymilk, cheese
     (optional)

Heat oven to 450 degrees. Scrub 4 large sized baking potatoes. Choose potatoes that are nice and long, about 6 inches, and about 3-4 inches tall. Poke a few random holes in them, and place in oven on the rack to bake. Let bake about 45 minutes. When they are done, carefully split them lengthwise. They are very hot! You can let them cool before cutting open, if that is easier. They'll cool fastest if you cut them first. I just hold them with a pot holder while I cut. The insides should be slightly undercooked, so that they seem a bit slick. Let the split potatoes cool while you prepare the stuffing. Turn the oven down to 350 degrees.

There are many variations you can enjoy, but here is a basic one.

In a mixing bowl, combine 1 small diced onion (you can substitute 4 scallions chopped), 1/2 green pepper chopped fine, 1/4 cup grated carrot, 1/4 cup finely chopped red cabbage, 1/2 bunch (about 8 leaves) greens, steamed or sauted in water until just wilted and reduced in volume or 1 cup frozen greens, thawed, chopped and excess water squeezed out, 2 cloves garlic, pressed or minced (optional), 1/4 cup small sized cooked bean (optional) such as lentils, mung, navy, or black beans, 1/4 cup nuts (pine nut, almond, or walnut) chopped small or 1/8 cup sunflower seeds raw or roasted, 1/4 cup yogurt or 1/4 cup milk or soymilk

When the above is well mixed, scoop out the insides of the cooled potatoes. Scoop out just enough to leave about a 1/4 inch shell, or a little more. You should have 8 shells. Divide the "insides" that you've removed in half. Store one half in a tight container, refrigerated or frozen, for future use to thicken soups, to add to a stir fry or casserole, etc. The remaining half needs to be mixed with the vegetable ingredients in your bowl. I use my hands, as the textures are sticky and uneven and hard to mix well with a spoon.

When that mixture is well mixed, scoop up spoonfuls (or again use your hands) and fill the hollowed potato shells. It is good to heap the filing to more than fill the shell, but not to much or it will fall out. As each one is finished, place on a baking sheet. For easy clean up, use parchment paper to line the cookie sheet or lightly oil or spray with a nonstick spray.

You can sprinkle a bit of grated cheese over each stuffed potato, sprinkle with a bit of olive oil, dust with paprika or just leave plain.

Bake at 350 degrees for 30 minutes.

You can freeze this by wrapping the individual stuffed potato in aluminum foil before the second baking. To reheat, the frozen stuffed potato can be heated in the foil for about 45 minutes at 350, unwrap it enough to expose just the top during the last 15 minutes.

Kale Balls

Use thawed frozen kale or 1 bunch kale chopped and steamed until just wilted. Combine in a medium bowl with 2 lightly beaten eggs, 1 cup bread crumbs, 1/2 t sage, 1/2 t thyme, 1 clove garlic minced, a pinch of salt or dash tamari, 1/4 cup freshly grated parmesan or romano cheese, 2 T olive oil.

Make small balls, about 1 inch in diameter. Place on greased cookie sheet, or use parchment paper. Bake 350 degrees for about 10-15 minutes until firm and just lightly browned.

> *Serves: makes about 16 balls*
> *Time: 15 minutes to prepare, 10-15 to bake*
> *Type of dish: snack or appetizer*
> *Equipment: basic, parchment paper really helps*
> *Leftovers: best eaten right away*
> *Ingredients: 1 bunch or 1 package frozen kale, eggs, bread crumbs, sage, thyme, garlic, olive oil, parmesan or romano cheese for grating*

The freshly grated parmesan is important to this recipe. It won't be as good if you use already grated cheese.

You can buy whole wheat bread crumbs or quickly make your own. Just take a few slices of bread, stacked. Slice into strips, then turn and slice again so you have tiny cubes. Spread them out in one layer on an ungreased cookie sheet. Bake at 350 for about 5 minutes, the time will vary depending on the bread so watch carefully. When they are crispy, and slightly browned, remove from oven. Opening the door just a crack frequently to check will let steam escape and that can help the process.

Smashed whole wheat crackers could be used in place of the bread crumbs.

Chard, collards, mache, lambs quarters, and other milder greens could be substituted for the kale.

Spanakopita Without Spinach

Serves: about 16 as
    appetizer
Time: 30 minutes to
    prepare, 30-40 minutes
    to bake
Type of dish: appetizer
Equipment: pastry brush,
    food processor or
    blender
Leftovers: once e it is
    cooked, eat right away.
Ingredients: 1 bunch
    yellow dock, dandelion,
    nettle, amaranth,
    lambs quarters or other
    wild green or spinach
    or mache or beet
    greens, or other mild
    conventional green,
    feta cheese, eggs, whole
    wheat phyllo dough,
    butter

Phyllo dough is usually sold frozen. Let it thaw at least 4-6 hours before you make this dish.

In a large skillet, saute in 2 T olive oil 1 medium to small onion, sliced thinly or use about 1/2 cup scallions thinly sliced. Add 1 bunch greens, or 1 package frozen. Yellow dock, dandelion, amaranth, nettle, and other wild greens alone or in combinations are great in this recipe. Cook until wilted and reduced in size, and water is evaporated.

Let cool slightly and place in blender or food processor with 2 eggs and pulse just so it is uniformly blended. Add another egg if the mixture is too thick. It should be thick like peanut butter, but able to be processed and mixed.

Melt a stick of butter in a small sauce pan.

Crumble 6 oz. of feta cheese into the food processor or blender. Pulse just enough to blend.

Quick and easy method: Lay a piece of phyllo dough into a 9 x 16 baking dish. It will be larger than the dish, for the first few layers just center the sheet and let it come up the sides. Lightly brush the whole sheet with melted butter. Don't soak it in butter, a little bit goes a long way. The phyllo should still have some dry spots, and not become gummy from too much butter.

Lay another piece of phyllo dough on top of the first. Brush with butter. Add three more sheets, with butter between, do not butter the last sheet. Spread 1/3 of the spinach mixture as thinly as possible but still cover most of the phyllo. Place another sheet of phyllo dough on top of that. Gently brush more butter on it (if the filling pokes through that's O.K.). Repeat phyllo sheet, butter, phyllo, etc. until you have four more layers. Spread half the remaining filling, cover that with four more layers of phyllo with butter between, and spread the rest of the mixture on that. Cover with 4 more sheets. This time, end with butter brushed on the last sheet. You can now carefully cut the edges removing the phyllo that is larger than the dish.

Bake at 350 for about 40 minutes, until top is golden brown.

There is also the flag fold method, for individual portions. This is a messy and labor intensive process. It is also my favorite. Begin by cutting the phyllo dough into about five pieces, before it is unfolded. Return four of the pieces to the plastic wrap. Unfold the section that remains. On a wooden cutting board or other work surface, place one of the sheets and brush with butter. Cover with another sheet of the dough.

Place about 1 T of the egg/greens/cheese mixture on one end of the strip. Flag fold (see illustration). Place on ungreased cookie sheet. Repeat until mixture is sed up, or you have used all your phyllo dough. Bake at 350 degrees for about 15 minutes, until browned and crispy. Let cool slightly and serve.

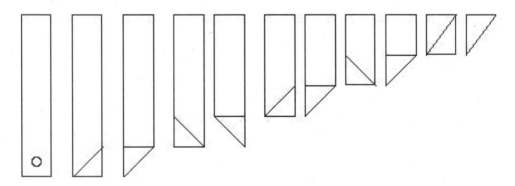

My first taste of spanakopita was baked by my high school boyfriend's grandmother. She was a wonderful cook and made all sorts of Greek delicacies for every family gathering. My favorites were spanakopita and tiropitakia. Tiropitakia is made similarly to spanakopita, but without the greens.
She taught me to make both, as well as other Greek pastries. I don't know what she would say about using weeds and whole wheat phyllo dough, but this recipe is included with fond memories of Yaya.

Tri-Level Mushroom and Greens Strudel

This is a fairly labor intensive, very rich and wild main course. The complexities of taste and texture make it very special, well worth the extra effort in preparation. There are no additional added seasonings, other than a touch of salt.

There are three layers to this strudel, with phyllo dough in between. Whole wheat phyllo dough can be purchased frozen in most health food stores. Everyone I know who has made their own phyllo has suggested that it is an experience not worth repeating.

Serves: 8
Time: 1 hour to prepare, 30 minutes to cook
Type of dish: main
Equipment: pastry brush, blender or food processor
Leftovers: does not freeze, leftovers the next day will be soggy but good
Ingredients: phyllo dough, three types of mushrooms, nuts, 1 bunch fresh or 1 package frozen greens, butter

To make the strudel you will prepare the three different layers of filling, and melt butter for the phyllo dough layers. The phyllo dough should be completely thawed, usually 24 hours in the refrigerator or 3-4 hours at room temperature will accomplish that.

To eliminate washing the skillet in between, I suggest you prepare the fillings in this order: nuts, mushrooms, and greens. A food processor will be helpful, a blender will pass, and in a pinch you can hand chop everything.

In a food processor, lightly pulse 2 1/2 cups of nuts. Almonds, walnuts, hazelnuts are all good choices, and can be combined. You could also add a small amount of pecans or pine nuts to these choices. Avoid stronger tasting nuts like cashews and non-nuts like peanuts and sunflower seeds. The mixture should be mostly still nut chunks, with some finer crumbs.

Heat a dry skillet. Add nut mixture and dry roast, by stirring constantly on medium high heat. As the nuts just begin to brown, remove from heat, scraping the pan with a wooden spoon, transfer roasted nuts to a bowl.

Slice 1 1/2 pounds of mushrooms, 1/2 pound each of three different types. I most commonly use shitake, moonlight, and portabella. You can vary this depending on what is available – morels, puffballs, chicken of the forest, porcini, chanterelles, are all good choices. The larger portabellas should be sliced and cut in half. It is best to have a variety of textures, so mushrooms that would cook similarly can be varied by slicing them thinner or thicker, or quartering in place of slicing.

Preheat the oven to 350 degrees.

Saute the mushrooms separately, using about 1 T olive oil each time. They should be lightly cooked, a minute or two, over medium heat, just so they begin to collapse, do not overcook. As you remove them from the skillet, use a second bowl to hold them. The mushrooms are mixed together after they are sauted separately.

Remove the pan from the heat while you prepare the greens. Use two bunches of greens, or 2 packages frozen. Swiss chard, collards, mild dandelions, spinach, are all good choices. I especially like collards and dandelion combined – 3/4 of the mixture being collards, and 1/4 dandelion.

If you are using fresh greens, wash and rinse, shake off the water and pat dry with a towel. Place in a food processor and in 2-3 batches pulse so that the greens are chopped fine. You can also do this in a blender, or by hand with a long knife.

If the greens are frozen, thaw them in advance. Put them in a food colander, and squeeze out excess water. The water you squeeze out can be saved for soups stock.

Without cleaning the skillet, add 3 T butter. Heat to medium high, and add greens as they fit, they will reduce in size so you can add more. Saute until they are wilted, reduced in size, and have turned bright green. Remove to a third bowl and set aside.

In a small sauce pan, melt a stick of butter. Remove the phyllo dough from the packaging and unroll. There are usually about 16 sheets per package, and this strudel needs four layers of phyllo. In a 9 x 14 inch shallow casserole dish lay one of the sheets of phyllo. It is OK if it comes up the sides a bit. Brush that sheet with melted butter, a pastry brush works well. Keep it light, but thorough, and be sure to go to the edges. Repeat – add a sheet, brush, until you have four sheets of phyllo with butter between. Do not brush the top sheet.

On that top sheet, spread the nut mixture evenly. Cover that with a sheet of phyllo, brush with butter, repeat until you have four more sheets of phyllo.

Carefully spread the green mixture over that sheet of phyllo. Cover with another sheet, brush with butter, and repeat as before until you have another four sheets.

On top of that, spread the mushroom mixture, It will work best if you spoon out the mushrooms first, then drizzle any remaining liquid over the mushrooms. If it seems too wet (more than a teaspoon of juice) reserve the juice for another use – it would be great just poured over grains or greens at another meal.

Lay the last four layers of phyllo as you did before, this time lightly brush the top as well.

Bake uncovered fro 30 minutes, until browned on top, serve right away or it can get soggy. Cut into approximately 3 inch squares, use a sharp knife to cut and serve with a spatula.

This recipe was inspired by a meal I had in a Seattle vegetarian restaurant. It combined a nut pate, mushroom mixture, and some vegetable in layers within a puff pastry. I loved the complex taste, the simplicity of the rich ingredients, and the combined textures. I knew I had to recreate it, because I don't get to Seattle all that often.
I was more familiar with phyllo than puff pastry, so I started with that and was so happy with the results I never even tried to more faithfully recreate the original inspiration.
This is a very rich treat, perfect for that extra special dinner party or celebration. It truly celebrates the satisfying taste of good ingredients.

Cabbage Rolls

Serves: 6-8
Time: 45 minutes to
        prepare, 45 minutes to
        bake
Type of dish: main
Equipment: large steamer,
        8 inch square casserole
        or similar
Leftovers: great as
        leftovers, and can be
        frozen
Ingredients: onion, garlic,
        mushrooms,
        buckwheat groats,
        sage, oregano, basil, 2
        cups chopped greens,
        one green cabbage,
        tomato sauce

In a sauce pan, saute 1 finely chopped onion in olive oil, add 2 cloves garlic minced or pressed. Cook about 3 minutes until tender. Add 1/4 pound mushrooms, sliced. Cook about 3 minutes until tender and add 2 cups buckwheat groats (kasha). Add 1/2 t each sage, oregano, and basil.

Add one quart water. Add two cups chopped greens. Spinach, kale, collards, chard, and wild greens are all good choices. Bring to boil, simmer 20 minutes or as long as it takes for water to be absorbed. To avoid burning, you can turn off the burner for the last 10 minutes and it will keep cooking.

While this mixture is cooking, core a large green cabbage. If you've never done this before, it is simple with a nice sharp knife. Make multiple deep (about two inch) cuts into the base of the cabbage. Angle the cuts so that you are aiming towards the very center of the cabbage. After about 5- 10 cuts the "core" (the harder broad stem like base) will pop out. Discard it, or save (freeze) for vegetable stock.

Steam the whole cored cabbage over boiling water until leaves are softened (about 15-20 minutes). Let cool and remove individual leaves with your fingers or with tongs.

Oil an 8 inch square baking dish. At the base of each cabbage leaf, place 2 T of the buckwheat and greens mixture. Roll up in the cabbage leaf, tucking in the sides of the leaf as you roll. Place seam side down in the dish.

Cover with 2 cups homemade or jarred spaghetti sauce, thinned with one cup water.

Bake 1 hour, at 350 degrees.

Creamed Greens

Serves: 4
Time: 15 minutes to prepare, 30 minutes to bake
Type of dish: side
Equipment: basic
Leftovers: reheats well, best to use within 3-5 days
Ingredients: 1 bunch greens fresh or 1 package frozen, whole wheat flour, butter, milk or milk, seasonings, bread crumbs

Grease a 10 inch square or similar round baking dish. In a large skillet, saute one bunch of greens ripped or chopped into bite sized pieces, with about 1/4 cup water or less. Use spinach, Swiss chard, collards, kale, mustard beet or turnip greens, or wild greens. Heat oven to 350 degrees. Cook greens 2-3 minute at most until just wilted and reduced in volume. Remove the greens from the skillet, using tongs may be easiest. Place the greens into the greased baking dish. If you use frozen greens, saute just long enough to break up the frozen pieces or thaw in advance.

Wipe skillet dry and clean with a cloth or paper towel. Make a roux. Melt 3 T butter. Just as it starts to sizzle, add 4 T whole wheat flour. Let cook a minute or two on medium to high heat, stirring a whisk is best. Add 2 cups milk (or fresh soy milk). Continue to cook on medium heat, stirring with a whisk. Within about 5 minutes it should start to thicken.

Once it begins to thicken, you can add seasonings.

Variations (choose only one): add salt and white pepper to taste (about 1/4 t each), stir in 1/2 cup grated cheddar or mild jack cheese, stir in 1-3 t Thai chili sauce. Stir in 1/4 cup sunflower seeds, stir in 1/4 cup tahini and 1 t lemon juice, stir in 1 T balsamic or other fancy vinegar.

Once you have the seasoning of your choice, let it slightly bubble for about a minute, stirring constantly. Pour cream sauce over spinach, mix lightly to have even distribution. If you have extra cream sauce, save for other uses (on pasta, grains, vegetables, etc.) Add whole wheat bread crumbs, OR crumbled bread and a dusting of paprika if desired.

Bake for 30 minutes.

Cream Cheese Green Cake

Serves: 6-8
Time: 20 minutes to
    prepare, 1 1/2 hours to
    bake, 3-4 hours to cool
    and chill
Type of dish: main
Equipment: spring form
    pan, grater, food
    processor
Leftovers: use within 2-3
    days, do not freeze
Ingredients: cracker
    crumbs, butter,
    parmesan cheese, olive
    oil, onion, mushrooms,
    cream cheese, eggs,
    carrots, 1 bunch greens
    or 1 package frozen,
    sour cream or cottage
    cheese

Combine about 4 oz. (1 cup) of cracker crumbs with 2 T butter and 1 T grated parmesan cheese in a food processor. Process until well mixed, add more butter if needed so that it sticks together when pinched. Press into the bottom of a spring form pan. Bake for 10 minutes in a 350 degree oven. Let cool.

While that is baking, saute one onion thinly sliced in 2 T olive oil. Add 1/2 pound mushrooms sliced thin. Shitake or moonlight mushrooms would both work well. Add 1 bunch fresh greens chopped or torn into bite sized pieces or 1 package frozen, thawed and water drained. Cook for about 5-10 minutes, until the greens are wilted and reduced in size. Remove from heat to cool.

In the same food processor container (no need to wash it from making the crust) cream 1 1/2 pounds cream cheese, 4 eggs, 1/4 cup sour cream or cottage cheese until light and fluffy.

Use a spatula to scrape this into a mixing bowl. Add the cooked mixture, and 1 cup grated carrots. Mix just enough to combine. Again using the spatula, fill the spring form pan with the mixture.

Bake for 1 1/2 hours at 300 degrees. Let cool for 1 hour, refrigerate until well chilled (2-3 hours) before removing the sides of the springform pan and serving.

Sandwiches, Wraps, Rolls and Dips

Lettuce is a staple for many sandwiches. You can use green leafy vegetables instead and boost the flavor and nutrition. This section will tell you how.

Tortillas, pitas and flatbreads can be used to scoop or wrap sandwich ingredients that include greens, grains, beans, and spreads. One recipe is included. You can also simply combine rice and beans topped with lightly steamed kale and a bit of salsa. Try a bit of leftover dal and rice with steamed chard. Steamed vegetables and greens with tahini spread on pita bread is a great quick meal. Leftovers and wraps are a natural combination.

A few appetizer ideas are also included in this section. Green leafy vegetables can begin to appear everywhere.

Garbanzo Bean Wrap

Serves: 4
Time: 20-30 minutes to
    cook if beans and
    grains are ready
Type of dish: main
Equipment: basic
Leftovers: best used within
    a day or two.
Ingredients: onion, olive
    oil, carrot, greens fresh
    or frozen, cumin,
    cooked or canned
    garbanzo beans, fresh
    or canned tomatoes,
    tahini, whole wheat
    flour tortillas

Saute in olive oil a medium onion, thinly sliced. When softened, add one medium size grated carrot and three cups chopped greens, mild or spicy. Or use one package frozen greens. Season with 2 t ground cumin, salt and pepper to taste. Cook on medium low for about 10 minutes.

Add one can garbanzo beans, or two cups well cooked beans , or use frozen beans you've previously cooked, thawed. Let everything heat well, greens have reduced in size and turned bright green. Then add two cups chopped fresh tomato, or add half can chopped tomato when you add in the garbanzo beans. If you mash some of the garbanzos with the back of your stirring spoon the sandwich will stick together better. Adding a couple T of Tahini will also help things stick together.

Add 1 cup pre-cooked rice, or combine 1/2 cup whole wheat bulgar with one cup boiling water, covered, let sit for 15 minutes.

Spoon generous amounts into warmed tortillas (use oven, grill, or cast iron pan to warm) and roll up. Flour tortillas roll more easily than corn. Serve warm, or refrigerate filling for later.

High protein foods go bad more quickly, so refrigerated beans will last 2-3 days. You can freeze garbanzos in small containers for quick and inexpensive additions.

Tempeh Salad Sandwich

Serves: 2
Time: 10 minutes to
    prepare, cooling time
Type of dish: main
Equipment: basic
Leftovers: keeps
    refrigerated for 2-3
    days does not freeze.
Ingredients: tempeh, olive
    oil, tamari,
    mayonnaise, onion,
    greens, sandwich
    bread.

Thinly slice an 8 oz. package of tempeh, and then chop so you have thin chunks. Heat 2 T olive oil in a skillet and add tempeh. Stir and cook over medium heat until slightly browned, about 5-10 minutes. Remove from heat once it has cooked and let cool.

When the tempeh has cooled mix it with 3 T mayonnaise, 1 t tamari, and 1/2 small onion, very thinly sliced.

Chill this for about an hour.

Steam 2 cups greens, any type, torn or chopped into large pieces or if using small leaved greens leave whole. They should be bright green, and wilted. Remove from steamer and chill.

When greens and tempeh mix is cold, place half the greens in a thick layer on a piece of whole grain bread. Spread half the tempeh salad on top of that, and top with another piece of bread, or leave open faced. Make the second sandwich with the rest of the ingredients.

The greens can also be uncooked, especially when using lambs quarters, chickweed, yellow dock, spinach, and chard.

Lightly steamed greens make a great addition to any salad where you might normally use lettuce. Try putting on a thicker layer than you might normally – 1/4 to 1/2 inch or more. Even a simple cheese sandwich comes alive with a pile of greens as thick as the cheese.

Toasting the bread improves the flavor of this sandwich.

Green Nori Rolls

Serves: 10-12
Time: 30-60 minutes to
    prepare once rice is
    coked and cooled
Type of dish: appetizer or
    main dish
Equipment: sushi mat
Leftovers: begins to dry out
    after a few hours, after
    a day the seaweed gets
    soggy.
Ingredients: rice, nori,
    greens, various
    vegetables (many
    choices)

Cook 2 cups rice, either brown sushi rice or short grain brown rice with a bit of extra water. Let cool. See how to cook rice at the end of this recipe.

Prepare the vegetables that will be rolled inside the rice and seaweed. They should all be sliced thinly, in long pieces. Use brightly colored ingredients. Include raw or lightly steamed (until just wilted) greens. If they are cooked, try and dry them from all excess water as much as possible by patting dry with a towel. Other options are carrots, red cabbage, beets (raw or pickled) daikon radish (raw, pickled or dried), watermelon radish, pickled or fresh burdock root, scallions, avocado slices, steamed asparagus, and cucumber.

Have Sushi Nori on hand, a package has 8-12 pieces. You will also need a sushi mat. This is a simple bamboo mat sewn together, about 9 inches square. An Asian specialty store should have them.

Prepare your work surface. Place the sushi mat on the surface, with the bamboo running horizontally. Put one sheet of sushi nori on the mat. With your fingers, place rice on the end of the nori closest to you, about 1/2 inch deep and extending about 1 1/2 inches from the end. Leave about a 1/4 – 1/2 inch border on the rice filled end.

Gently place strips of vegetables you've prepared on the rice. Use the greens last, so that the other vegetables will show when you cut the nori later.

At this point you have some options. You may want to place some seasoning in the nori, you may want to serve the seasoned sauces on the side. Possible internal seasonings include a mayo/ wasabi sauce, ume plum paste (available in the Asian section of most health food stores), pickled ginger, and tamari with or without wasabi. I prefer the seasonings on the side. Not only so that you have a choice with each piece, but also so that people can choose how hot they will enjoy their nori rolls. I also find that nori rolls will be less soggy without sauces. If you want a sauce, spread it gently on top of the greens.

Start to rolling the mat and the nori containing the rice away from you. The important step here is to tuck that non-rice filled border in as you roll the creation. Roll it as tight as possible, using the mat to apply even pressure. Have a dish of water handy to apply a line of water lightly to the end of the nori farthest from you, that will seal the roll. Pat the ingredients that may be protruding from each open end, and set aside.

Repeat for each roll.

Cutting the rolls into the traditional circles is a delicate process. You really need to use a sharp serrated knife. Apply as little pressure as possible. I stabilize the roll with a finger on either side of the cut. Don't start your cut on the seam. Frequently, the first piece is mashed and you can snack on it.

Arrange the sliced pieces on a large tray, and serve with dipping sauce on the side.

The Sauces:

Wasabi comes as a paste, or as a powder. It is a very hot, pungent rhizome that is a traditional Japanese condiment.

> Ingredients for sauces and
>   accompaniments:
>   tamari, wasabi paste
>   or powder,
>   mayonnaise, honey,
>   lemon juice, ume
>   plum paste, pickled
>   ginger

Wasabi-joyu

When mixed with soy sauce, wasabi is called Wasabi-joyu. Put a couple of T of tamari in a small dish, and slowly adding wasabi, to taste. How much will vary depending on the taste of those who will be consuming it.

Simple Wasabi Mayonnaise

Wasabi mayonnaise is made similarly, by slowly adding wasabi paste or powder to mayonnaise to taste.

Wasabi Mayonnaise

For a fancier version, combine 1 cup mayonnaise, 1 T tamari, 1 t honey, 2 t lemon juice, 2 t wasabi paste, or 1 t powder

Pickled ginger is a traditional accompaniment, available in health food stores or specialty stores. A dot of ume plum paste can also be served on the side.

How to cook rice – In a large sauce pan combine 4 cups water with 2 cups brown rice. Cover and bring to a boil. Let it simmer about 20 minutes. Turn off the heat, and let the pan sit still covered for 20 minutes. Do not stir until the rice is cooked and the water is absorbed.

Green dip

Serves: 12-16
Time: 15 minutes to steam, mix, and 30 minutes to chill.
Type of dish: dip
Equipment: food processor or blender
Leftovers: will keep for up to 3 days, do not freeze.
Ingredients: greens, cream cheese, sour cream, garlic, hot sauce, parmesan or romano cheese, miso.

Use fresh or frozen greens, about 2 cups, that have been thawed or lightly steamed. Pulse in a food processor or blend long enough to chop fine. Mix into 1 package cream cheese, 1 cup sour cream, 2 cloves of garlic pressed, a dash of your favorite hot pepper sauce, 1/2 cup grated parmesan or ramono cheese, 1 T miso.

Mix well and chill for at least 30 minutes to blend flavors. Serve with crackers, or as a vegetable dip.

Clancy's Fancy Hot Sauce is a great addition to this dip, as well as to many of the soups and other dishes. It is made locally – in Ann Arbor, Michigan.

Green Dipping Sauce

Serves: 10-12
Time:: about 20 minutes to pepare and 2-3 hours to chill.
Type of dish: dip
Equipment: basic
Leftovers: use within 2 days, do not freeze
Ingredients: 1/2 bunch fresh or 1/2 package frozen greens, parsley, tarragon, mayonnaise or yogurt

Prepare 1/2 bunch of greens, or 1/2 package greens. Swiss chard, collard, spinach, watercress, are all good choices and can be combined as well. If using fresh wash and chop fine. If using frozen, chop as they are unthawing.

Saute in a bit of water over medium heat until just softened, about 5-10 minutes depending on the greens used. Remove from heat and drain (reserve liquid for soup stock). Add 1/4 cup parsley finely chopped and 2 T fresh tarragon. Let cool a few minutes and add to 1 1/2 cups mayonnaise or yogurt

Refrigerate 2-3 hours before serving.

Extras

A few of the recipes didn't fit under the previous sections.

Greens for Your Animals

Your pets can also benefit from including dark green leafy vegetables. If your dog doesn't enjoy raw or steamed greens added to their food, try these treat recipes. I haven't yet found a dog who doesn't love them. Cats prefer the simplicity of home grown grass. A handful of grass seed will last most of the winter, just sow a bit more every week or two in a small shallow container.

Vinegar Infusions

Vinegar is important to greens. Vinegar can increase the absorption of the minerals from greens, adds to the flavor, and vinegar infusions are another way to use greens in your diet.

Blanching and Freezing

Hopefully you will find yourself with more greens than you can eat. Buying in season and freezing on your own is a way to ensure you have greens all winter. Wild greens as well as ones you've grown are reminders of the growing season when you enjoy them midwinter and at other times. Here is how to make it quick and easy.

Additional Ideas

A few thoughts on other dishes that can be enhanced by greens.

Zomba's Yam Garlic Treats

THESE TREATS ARE FOR DOGS

In a food processor, mix 1 cup yogurt with 3 cloves peeled whole garlic and one slightly chopped unpeeled raw sweet potato.

Add 1 egg, 1 T olive oil, a pinch of salt, and approximately 2 cups whole grain flour such as whole wheat, corn, spelt, buckwheat, or other or a combination of any of these. Oatmeal can also be used. Process about two minutes so it is well mixed.

Serves: enough treats for two dogs for a week and some left over to freeze
Time: 10 minutes to prepare, 2 hours to bake
Type of dish: dog treat
Equipment: cookie press helps a lot
Leftovers: freeze in small bags, will keep at east a week refrigerated
Ingredients: yogurt, garlic, egg, olive oil, whole grain flour, sweet potato, greens.

The quick and easy method is to use the dough that is not very thick, place it in a cookies press, and use one of the roundish nozzles and squirt long strings onto a cookie sheet. Bake about 2 hours or more in a slow (250 degree) oven until brown and crispy all through. Break into small pieces, cool, and refrigerate. Using parchment paper on the cookie sheets makes clean up even easier.

To roll the treats instead of using a cookie press transfer the dough from the food processor to a mixing bowl and add enough flour to form a thick batter. Roll out to 1/4 inch thickness and cut. The dough needs to be stiff and this will take more time.

For a more "cookie like" texture, add 1/2 baking powder with the flour.

I made up this recipe after seeing how much my dogs love sweet potatoes. Adding the greens gives it an even greater nutritional boost, and I haven't found a dog yet who doesn't love these treats. We've given them away, with the recipe, to the dogs we've taken classes with.
So many of the dog treat recipes I found are so labor intensive. Using the cookies press I can have these made and in the oven within ten minutes. My dogs can still eat these faster than I can make them. I often double the recipe and freeze small bags for later.

Ambo's Green Cheese Treats

*Serves: enough treats for
two dogs for a week
and some left over to
freeze*
*Time: 10-20 minutes to
prepare, 2 hours to
bake*
Type of dish: dog treat
*Equipment: cookie press
helps a lot*
*Leftovers: freeze in small
bags, will keep at east a
week refrigerated*
*Ingredients: yogurt, whole
grain flour, egg, olive
oil, cheese, greens,
oatmeal*

THESE TREATS ARE FOR DOGS

In a food processor or blender combine 2 cups whole grain flour, 1/2 t baking powder, 1/2 cup yogurt, 1 egg, 1/2 cup grated cheese, 1 T olive oil, 2 cups greens fresh or frozen (if using frozen allow to thaw press to remove excess water). Blend, and add oatmeal as needed to make a thick dough.

Line a cookie sheet with parchment paper, or grease well. Drop small tea-spoon sized balls onto the cookie sheet, close together. Or add a little liquid to the dough and use a cookie press to make lines of dough that you then score to easily break apart. Bake at 200 degrees for about two hours, until lightly browned and crispy.

Infused Vinegars

Vinegar is a great solution for gaining and preserving the nutrients and taste from an herb or dark green leafy vegetable. When vinegar is part of a meal, or sprinkled on greens, it increases your mineral absorption from the greens.

Infused vinegars are easy to make, and versatile in how you use them. Most of us are familiar with fancy flavored vinegars with a sprig or two of an herb. Well, that is the idea but this is with a whole lot more of the plant.

A simple herbal or green vinegar is made by picking healthy greens and/or herbs, preferably from your garden, but in a pinch store bought will do. Simply chop the greens to expose more surface area, place in a clean glass jar, pour in organic apple cider or organic white vinegar, and cover with a non metal lid. Label the jar, and let it sit for 6 weeks in a dark cool place.

At the end of 6 weeks, strain out the liquid and store in a glass jar (again no metal lid), and discard the greens. The result is calcium and mineral rich with absorption enhanced by the vinegar.

I learned to make herbal vinegars from Susun Weed. In her book, "Menopausal Years the Wise Woman Way" one of her infused vinegar recipes provides 150-200 mg. of calcium per tablespoon. The amount of calcium will vary depending on the plants you use and how full the jar is with greens, but that gives you some idea how rich in calcium an infused vinegar can be.

These vinegars are great for drizzling on rice or other grains, in casseroles, as an ingredient in salad dressing (just use in place of regular vinegar), or even as a nutritional boost by mixing a tablespoon or two in water and drinking. I use it as a bed time aid, a tablespoon in a 1/2 cup of water helps me to sleep because of the high calcium content.

Use the leaves from these wild plants for a rich and tasty infusion: lambs quarters, dandelion, raspberry, nettle, plantain, yellow dock, and chickweed. You can also infuse kale and collards, the fresher the better.

Vinegars can also be made from parts you might normally discard. Chive blossoms make a beautiful and tasty vinegar. I use white vinegar so the beautiful pink color really shows. Susun also taught me to use the stems from shitake mushrooms in a vinegar. They tend to be too tough to cook with anyway. The result really tasty to use in dressings and bakes, and full of the nutritional benefits mushrooms provide.

Simply remove the stems, chop them a little, and place in a small jar with apple cider or organic white vinegar. Let sit for six weeks, and strain out the mushrooms.

In addition to a range of herbal infusions, other vinegars you might want to have on hand include:

balsamic
red wine
white wine
apple cider
a fruit vinegar
rice vinegar
white vinegar

There are vast differences in white vinegars, and it took me years to find one that was suitable for tasting and not cleaning. Be careful what you select, it is hard to tell the difference just from the ingredients on the label. I found one made by the same company as other natural food products and it is very good.

Blanching for Freezing

Most green plants need to be blanched before being frozen. Bring water to boil in a fairly large pot. While waiting for it to boil, pick through the greens. Remove center ribs if they are tough. Watch for stay insects, and leaves with eggs, remove or discard. Rinse the leaves, set aside until you have a large pile. When the water comes to a boil, place your pile of leaves into the water, so that they are all submerged. In about 30 seconds the leaves will turn a brighter shade of green.

Remove with tongs, and pack freezer bags, or plastic containers, with the greens. Use somewhat small containers so that you will have just a portion or two of greens in each container. As you choose freezer containers, you can measure the greens so that you can easily incorporate them into recipes. A pint as is a standard measurement in many recipes (equal to a 10 oz. package of frozen greens).

Most instructions for blanching will tell you to plunge the cooked greens into cold water. I have always skipped this step, with no ill effects. The key is to only lightly cook the greens, package small amounts so they freeze quickly, and get them into the freezer right away. These frozen greens are best used within about six months, they begin to lose more substantial nutritional value after that time.

It helps to have two types of frozen greens on hand. Whole leaves, or only slightly torn, and chopped greens. For the larger leaved kale and collards, just tear a few times as you put handfuls into the boiling water. If you work quickly you can do it as you add them, if you're slower tear them all in advance and add at once. For the chopped greens blanch them whole, and as I remove them from the boiling water, put them right into a food processor. When the container is half full, I pulse it a few times, and scoop the more macerated result into my freezer container. These chopped greens are perfect for quick additions to recipes including burritos, lasagna, late additions to soups, stir fries, on homemade pizza, and more.

Additional Ideas

If you're new to greens, if you're trying to feed kids, if you just don't want to know that the greens are in there, you can hide the taste easily.

Green vegetables can be easily added to food, and it is a good habit to get into. As you eat more, you will probably start to enjoy the actual taste more and more. But in the meantime, there is no need to deprive yourself of the great nutritional benefits!

There are also any number of foods that can be adapted to include dark green leafy vegetables. It's just a matter of getting into the habit of using them, and also having greens readily available both fresh and frozen so that you can easily include them.

Chopped and steamed greens can be added to homemade pizza. When you make a burrito or enchilada include chopped greens with the beans. Potato salad tastes great with raw or steamed and chilled greens in bite sized pieces. Lasagna often includes spinach, use other greens as well and increase the amount.

Use a variety of greens in your next omelette. Crepes are a natural container for greens by themselves, with cheese and onions. Most crepe fillings can have greens added to them. Incorporate greens into souffles and other baked dishes.

With imagination, the recipes and ideas in this book, and a desire to enjoy them, you can eat dark green leafy vegetables every day and always be eating something new and interesting - that also tastes great.

Loving Life and Dark Green Leafy Vegetables

Enchanted with plants

My parents were gardeners. We always had herbs, vegetables, flowers and trees that we planted and nurtured. I knew where tomatoes came from. I helped put manure on the plants as a young girl. I grew up playing in open fields and meadows. My mother was passionate about wild flowers. She wasn't a very active person, but in the spring she came to life and we would take numerous hikes to see her favorite wild flowers. I learned them well enough that I could lead hikes for the Brownie and Girl Scout troops. I loved the plants so much that when my favorite open field was threatened with development I organized my friends to stop it. I was just ten years old, and that victory helped set me on my path. Nature was preserved.

Although the plants were a part of me, there was a disconnection about plants as food. We had vegetables every night for dinner, and some did come from the garden. But when I was growing up our salads always tasted the same – iceberg lettuce, peeled cucumber slices, wedges of tomato, and bottled dressing. The vegetables were equally bland. Every night my mother would pull a square box of frozen vegetables from the freezer — most often broccoli, peas, or corn (with the occasional lima bean or something equally exotic). She had a small eight inch square casserole dish, she would put a half inch of water in the pan, a pinch of salt, add the frozen vegetable that fit the pan exactly, and cook it on the stove top. That was vegetables for five.

After I left home I became a vegetarian. There were a few problems with my initial embracing of vegetarian concepts. First, the rejection of a whole category of food is not the basis of a good diet. There has to be more to it than that. Second, my creativity with cooking reverted to early training — to make it exotic and interesting melt cheese on it. I really had no idea what vegetarianism could be. The idea of a "plant based" diet was still a foreign concept to me. The vegetarian roommate who inspired me to change ate tofu and peanut butter sandwiches for nearly every meal. Not the best role model.

Luckily, I lived in a community of people who knew more than I did. I joined the Ann Arbor People's Food Co-op (PFC) in 1980. Like so many Co-ops around the country the PFC has always been an inspiration for good health, good food and, of course, debate about what should we eat and what are the consequences of doing so. In every part of town there are stores where fabulous produce is available and more and over time more of it is also organic.

In 1981 I lived for two months in a vegetarian community on Orcas Island, near Seattle, Washington. While doing work exchange in the kitchen, as well as eating three meals a day of inspired vegetarian food, I began to understand how to bring green plants to life — so that they were truly enjoyable to eat. The kitchen staff was aware of the atmosphere, and kept things positive and fun.

My education took a big leap when I met herbalist and author Susun Weed. Through Susun, I reconnected with the wild plants of my youth and found out that many of them were food! Incorporating "weeds" into my diet seems like second nature to me now, and indeed I think it is a natural thing for all of us. We've just been trained out of it.

Once I learned about the abundance of wild food around me my choices for vegetables and greens exploded. Now, when I see a lawn seeded with dandelions, with plantain in rosettes, chickweed visible with tiny flowers, and other greens poking out through the monotonous grass I think YUM! Luckily, more and more people are now realizing that basic simple nourishment is everywhere – literally growing at our feet.

Nourishment and Transformation

The nutritious green plants that surround us are a minor miracle. They contain nutrients critical to preserving our health. Calcium, for example, is something we can't live without. It is in every green plant. Carotenes, antioxidants, minerals, they are all there in quantities that have a significant positive impact on every aspect of our health. These are foods that truly fight disease, and help to preserve our health.

Nourishment can be the most challenging gift we give to ourselves. So much of what passes for healing is actually closer to punishment. People focus on what is bad for us, rather than what helps. Even the rather advanced concept of disease prevention and wellness is more about what to avoid rather than what to take in. We're bombarded with scary stories, ominous research, and cautionary tales.

The choice to include dark green leafy vegetables is practicing nourishment at a very simple and basic level. They taste good, it feels good, and your body responds in a positive way. And when you choose to nourish yourself, you're choosing life. A longer, healthier, happier life.

When you have the experience of being surrounded by healthy, life giving, good tasting plants, the world is a more friendly and supportive place. The adventure of finding wild food is a connection with the earth that so many people have lost, and crave at a very deep level. The simple act of regularly adding dandelions to your salad connects you to the seasons, to the environment around you, to awareness of who is poisoning their lawns and who is nourishing their environment. When you spend time picking dandelions, you're out in the yard, like you were as a kid, noticing what is at your feet, letting your mind wander perhaps a bit more than usual.

It is very simple, and potentially very transformative.

Developing a Philosophy

For more than thirty years I have carefully asked questions and listened to people talk about their dietary choices. What I hear, overwhelmingly, is what people are trying to avoid, trying to cut down on, trying to eliminate. It is a rare case when someone responds to my questioning by describing what they love to eat, what nourishes them, and the good parts of their diet.

What to eat, what to avoid, what to minimize, are topics of extreme passion for some, confusion for others. My observation from thousands of interviews is that most people carry massive guilt about food, and only achieve their ideals by punitive self-control. Some indulge in self-righteousness, some in appalling denial.

From all of this listening, studying, my own research and careful consideration I've learned what is the "best" diet. It is to eat more nourishing food. Focus on adding healthier food and the rest more easily falls away. And what food is most needed, most desirable, most nutritious, and most ignored by so many? Dark green leafy vegetables.

What we choose to eat reflects our experience with food as kids, where we live in the world, our finances, our free time, the season of the year, our inborn tastes, if we're eating with other people (especially kids) and trying to address their needs, +special dietary needs due to health challenges or disease, our emotional health, and even as personal an issue as how well and how long it takes us to digest food.

There will always be a continuum of lifestyles and choices.

Gain knowledge

Compared to even a few years ago, there is a wealth of scientific knowledge we can learn and use. Nutrition is now gaining recognition as a vital factor in disease prevention and health maintenance. We need to read between the lines on articles and reports of nutritional findings. Otherwise they will only create more confusion. There are so many sources for good information, beware of those who are selling just one approach and their own line of "must have" products. Both short and long term benefits are important as many aproaches give an immediate boost that doesn't last.

Nutrition is also nothing new. There is a lot of wisdom in returning to earlier knowledge and understanding of what is good to eat. Unprocessed food, grains, wild greens, local food, and eating in season are not new ideas but rather how we developed and evolved over thousands of years as human beings. The last fifty years have brought radical and unprecedented shifts in diet and consumption, with no accompanying change in our ability to adapt.

Never before has diet been so driven by advertising. Never before have food choices been so broad including overwhelming amounts of sugar and fat. These offerings are designed to capitalize on our innate need for energy to survive when times are lean, not every day for months and years on end.

We have gained knowledge of modern food safety and lost knowledge of some of the traditional basics of simple food.

Practice nourishment

For many people it is a complete reversal of the thought process to consider what nourishes their body, rather than fighting to eliminate what harms. It takes practice to continually (and soon habitually) choose healthy food that deeply nourishes the body.

How could a "health" regime that emphasizes purging, cleansing, and seeming punishment be healthy? On every level, we crave nourishment. With nourishmnet our bodies can heal and function optimally – taking care of the cleansing, balancing and health building we need. Our bodies function well when they are nourished.

Gain Awareness

What we eat has an immediate effect on how we feel. Our bodies need constant nourishment, and the immediate and long term affects of dietary choices will become apparent. Simple awareness of what we eat, when we eat it, and how we feel afterwards, will provide you with abundant information and feedback so that you can make good choices.

Awareness also extends to the impact of farming and agricultural practices around us, and around the world. What are the true costs of having raspberries in February? What impact does exportation of food have on some of the more fragile environments? What happens when farm animals are routinely fed antibiotics? The questions and possible areas of concern may feel overwhelming.

Greater awareness allows for greater participation, authentic feeling, motivation to work for change, and the ability to make better choices.

Have compassion

We're not perfect beings, and our choices are not always the best. Viewing the world with compassion allows us to experience peace. It takes practice, it takes patience. It even takes commitment.

Food and food politics are subjects we encounter every day, all day long. Every time we eat, every time we see a commercial, every time we shop we are confronted with food, and even our entertainment revolves around food. During emergencies food is one of the immediate needs. Any disruption of farming and distribution can lead to a crisis. Food is constant and it is overarching.

Which means the opportunity to practice compassion, understanding, and acceptance of our choices and the choices of others is also constant.

My experience is that compassion goes further in helping us make better choices than guilt, fear, and punishment. And if you mix in some fun, laughter, and pleasure - anything is possible.

Make connections

Connections with food can be made at many levels. Maybe it is who cooked it for you. Maybe it is a meal that simply includes your favorite foods. You may have the luxury of knowing the person who grew the food, or you may have picked the fruit yourself, or found the greens on a walk through the woods.

It's all about connection. The stories, the knowledge, the background, all add substance to what you eat. When food comes to us from places uknown, unseen, and unfelt we have lost a part of what can be truly special and fun about what we consume. Maybe you can reclaim it by making it into a favorite dish for someone. Better yet, find out something about how it was grown, who has been a part of the process, and how it came to be on your table.

Connecting with our food, knowing the source, even to the point of being involved in the growing and harvesting and preparing and finally eating, is a part of what we as humans have always done. It feels good to return to that.

Set priorities

Many people try and make abrupt, total, and radical dietary changes all at once. It is a style that only works for a few people. For most of us, finding one or two top priorities, focusing on those, and having compassion for the rest, is more likely to succeed. For many of my clients and friends, the simple priority of adding more dark green leafy vegetables to their diet has been a great start to more healthy and enjoyable eating.

The great thing about adding to your diet (rather than withholding or withdrawing) is that it feels good, and the things that aren't as good for you often just fall away. Your interest in sweet, salty, fatty foods may decrease when you are really happy and satisfied with a pile of tasty greens.

When you set a few priorities, rather than total and sudden change, you increase the chance of success, and the positive reinforcement that it brings.

What we eat does matter

Our diet affects our health. Some of us are more vulnerable to poor dietary choices than others. Some of us truly need "dietary recovery" to bring us back to health, or to slow the progression of disease.

In nearly all cases, the addition of dark green leafy vegetables will be of benefit. The rest of the puzzle - all the questions about what to eat and what to avoid, how to tailor your diet to your best health - are beyond the scope of this book, and much too individual to be able to adequately cover in a few hundred pages.

How to get more individual help

Dietary questions are unique, just as dietary preferences should be. There is no one right approach, or person, for all questions. You're more likely to get help from someone who has more than one approach, who listens to and respects your values, and is not simultaneously giving you advice and selling you the solution. Merge science and evidence with your gut feeling, and know that you're not alone in needing more help.

• Your concerns may be in the scientific, factual nutrition realm. A nutritionist or dietician may be the answer.

• You may have a physical problem causing digestive problems. A medical doctor or other health professional should be consulted.

• Your problem may be behavioral, or emotional. A therapist, especially one knowledgeable about eating disorders, may be the best option.

• You may have philosophical or value questions about your diet. These concerns may be best addressed by talking with friends, spiritual advisors, exploring ideas through lectures and workshops, or by reading.

 • Your problem may be one of finding the right foods, and learning about what is available. Your local co-op, natural foods store, farmer's market, or mail order catalogs for natural foods may all be resources.

 • You may be looking for more good recipes and inspiration. Look for social groups organized around certain food choices, or start a dinner group of your own. If your local newspaper has a recipe column, ask for help there. Cooking classes are widely available, and are even being offered at hospitals and health centers.

Glossary of Unusual Ingredients

Asafetida
This resin is in the parsley family and is a pungent spice used in Indian and Middle Eastern cooking. It should be cooked in hot oil to bring out the flavor. Powdered asafetida is mixed with rice flour, and is much less potent than the pure form. The powder is used in all recipes in this book. Asafetida is found in Asian groceries and specialty stores.

Buckwheat Groats
Buckwheat kernels are hulled to make buckwheat groats. Kasha is another name for buckwheat groats. Buckwheat is related to Rhubarb. A common variety is Fagopyrum esculentum, and there are other types.

Bulgur
Bulgur is made by cooking and then cracking wheat. Because it is pre-cooked, it is quickly prepared.

Jerusalem Artichoke
Jerusalem Artichoke (Helianthus tuberosus) is also known as the sunchoke. Jerusalem artichokes contain high levels of inulin, allowing them to be starch free and very few calories according to Organic Gardening Magazine. They are also high in iron. These earthy tubers can be eaten raw, cooked in soups, used as potato substitutes in many recipes, added to stir fries, and more. Once established they tend to overwhelm a garden.

Miso
Miso is a soybean paste that has been injected with a mold (koji culture) aged anywhere from 6 months to 3 years. It can be light or dark, with the lighter varieties having a milder taste. Miso can also contain other ingredients in addition to the soy.

Nori
One of the most processed of seaweeds, nori is available in flat sheets that are used to make sushi or nori rolls.

Phyllo Dough
This is a very thin pastry used in many Middle Eastern recipes. Whole wheat phyllo is available. It is usually found in the freezer section of food stores. It must be thoroughly thawed before using. This takes about 3-4 hours at room temperature, or 24 hours in the refrigerator. It easily dries out while you are working with it, so only remove from the plastic wrap as much as you will use right away.

Polenta

Dried corn is ground to make the fine flour used to make polenta. The quality of the polenta will vary depending on the corn, the method used to grind it, and its freshness. Freshly ground cornmeal using stone to grind it is especially recommended.

Quinoa

A grain used by the Incas, Quinoa is especially prized for its high protein content. Cooked like any other grain, it must be rinsed carefully or it will have a bitter taste. Use 2 cups water for 1 cup quinoa, cook for about 15-20 minutes.

Risotto

Risotto is an Italian rice cooked by slowly adding water or broth. Normally it is made from Arborio rice.

Tahini

Tahini is made from roasted or raw sesame seeds. In stores it is usually found with peanut butter, and other nut butters.

Tamari

Soy sauce and tamari are different, although both have s salty flavor. Tamari is made from soybeans, while soy sauce is made from wheat and soybeans. Both are fermented. The wheat can cause the fermentation to be sharper and more like alcohol. Some soy sauces are not fermented and are made from hydrolyzed vegetable protein. These are not traditional aged sauces, and have a very different and somewhat unpleasant flavor as well as lacking the nutritional value of tamari and soy sauce. Tamari is available at Asian specialty and natural food stores.

Tempeh

Tempeh is made from soybeans that have been cooked and injected with culturing agent and then allowed to sit for a day or more. The result is a soy product that can be used in stir fries, marinated and grilled, baked, and included in many recipes. It is a good source of protein. Tempeh is said to have originated over 2,000 years ago in Indonesia. It is available frozen or refrigerated at most natural foods stores. Some supermarkets are now carrying it.

Ume Plum Paste and Vinegar

Ume plum is a tangy fermented product made from umeboshi plums. It is often combined with red shisho leaf. The result is an intriguing sour flavor that goes well with grains, and other foods. It is commonly available as a paste, as whole plums, and as a vinegar. Most Asian specialty and natural food stores carry it.

Wasabi

Wasabi is in the mustard family and is an evergreen crucifer. While all parts of the plant can be used, the rhizome is a source for much of the powder and pastes that are sold. When you buy wasabi, make sure it is listed as one of the primary ingredients. Wasabi may have medicinal value as well, and there is ongoing research. Asian specialty and natural food stores will carry it.

Index of greens

Index of recipes

About the Author

Linda Diane Feldt lives in Ann Arbor, Michigan with her two Rhodesian Ridgeback dogs. She has maintained a full time private practice in integrated holistic health for more than two decades, and teaches classes and workshops locally and nationally.

A student of the healing arts since 1973, her work includes Polarity Therapy, Cranialsacral Therapy, massage therapy, and herbology. Linda Diane is the author of <u>Massage: Learning to Give and to Receive</u> and <u>Dying Again: Thirteen Years of Writing and Waiting</u>.

At the time of this publication, Linda Diane is an active hospice volunteer providing pet therapy, President of the Board of Directors of The People's Food Co-op, a volunteer teacher for the Ann Arbor Public Schools Community High School Community Resource Program, and she offers a free monthly class on herbal wisdom through the People's Food Co-op.